Retreats for Teens
Planning Strategies and Teen-Tested Models

Debbie Olla

Pflaum Publishing Group
Dayton, OH 45439
800-543-4383
www.Pflaum.com

Retreats for Teens
Planning Strategies and Teen-Tested Models

Interior Design by Patricia Lynch

Cover Design by Larissa Thompson

Second printing: 2002

ISBN 0-937997-78-1
3213

Contents

Dedication

To the memory of Father Tom Tearney, lovingly called "FT,"
    for planting the seeds of my faith and cultivating the soil,

To the young people with whom I have experienced retreats,
    for teaching me so much,

To the volunteer leaders at Mary Queen of Heaven and St. Dominic,
    for the honor and privilege of working with them,

To my family and friends,
    for encouraging me and praying for me and my ministry.

Acknowledgements

A special thank-you to....

all the young people and retreat team members I have worked with, especially from Mary Queen of Heaven Parish, West Allis, WI, and St. Dominic Parish, Brookfield, WI. Their ideas and suggestions have improved and enhanced the retreats.

to the National Evangelization Teams (NET), St. Paul, MN. Many of the things I learned through my training and experiences with NET are woven into this book.

to Kieran Sawyer, SSND, director of the Tyme Out Retreat Center, Nashotah, WI. She has given me inspiration and opportunities to continue to work in retreat ministry.

Introduction

Welcome to a very exciting, high-impact adventure in youth ministry. Retreats* can provide some of the most important faith moments in a person's life. Countless people have had life-changing experiences during a retreat. Maybe you are one of those people.

When we put our energies into planning and directing a retreat, we are hoping that those who participate will be touched by and come to know God in a deeper and more personal way. Makes you want to dive right in, doesn't it? But wait! You'll need to do some planning. And this book can help.

The most important steps in planning, creating, and executing a quality retreat are PRAYER, PRAYER, and PRAYER. I cannot emphasize this enough. We must begin in prayer; the heart of our planning must be prayer; and the execution of the retreat must include prayer, and so must living out the experience.

Let's begin.

Lord Jesus,

We come to you in this moment asking for your guidance in our retreat work. Guide us through the power of the Holy Spirit. Help us to be instruments for your plan so that all we do will glorify your name. We pray, as we pray all things, in the name of Jesus our brother.

Amen

*The word *retreat* will be used throughout this book to refer to any type of retreat experience, from a three-day overnight to a two-hour time of reflection, and anything in between.

The Five Ws and One H for Planning a Retreat

A retreat is time away, a withdrawing from worldly activities for spiritual recollection, study, and fellowship. It's a *retreat* from ordinary routines and surroundings to regroup, reenergize, and to experience and celebrate faith.

Retreats for young people generally focus on themes that relate to experiences in their lives. The primary goal is to help teens step away from normal daily life to focus on their spiritual growth and to integrate faith with lived experiences.

To develop an effective retreat for young people, it is important to do some groundwork. Begin by asking the five Ws and one H—Who? What? Why? Where? When? and How?

WHO?

The question Who? has two parts. First, Who is the target group or audience? Is it the ninth-grade youth group? Or is it everyone who participates in the high school youth ministry program? Or is it a group of parents and teens? Deciding whom you are preparing the retreat for will help you meet the needs of the group. Where are they spiritually? What are their faith needs?

The second part of the question is, Who is needed to make this retreat happen? Your list may include a guest speaker, someone to share a witness talk, a person to be in charge of the food, small group leaders, and other adult helpers. The list you make here will probably change and take shape as you answer the other questions.

Each retreat experience is unique because the Who?—who is the target group, and who is helping— is different. Each person brings his or her own personality and faith experiences to the retreat. So even if you did a retreat on peer pressure last year, this year's will be different because the Who? has changed.

WHY?

Why would this group benefit from a retreat? Does this group need to have a retreat experience as part of their preparation for Confirmation? Or would a retreat help to build community within a newly formed youth group?

WHAT?

The question What kind of retreat should be offered? has three parts.

1. Theme

What theme is appropriate for the target group? Preparing for Confirmation? Understanding and maintaining relationships? Building community? Strengthening family?

2. Purpose and Objectives

What is the purpose for having this retreat? The objectives will flow out of the purpose. If the purpose of the retreat is to improve communication between parents and teens, the objectives may be to present guidelines for effective communication and to give families opportunities to practice using these guidelines.

3. Format

What will be the most effective format for the retreat? Should the retreat involve a couple of hours, the better part of a day, or an entire weekend? Should it include an overnight?

WHEN?

Answering the question When? involves looking at the target group and discovering what else is competing for participants' attention and time. School? Parish life? Community involvement? Jobs? Sports? You would not want to plan a family retreat for the evening when parent/teacher conferences are scheduled in the parish school or local school district. Obviously, you would not schedule a retreat for high school juniors on the weekend of the high school formal dance.

WHERE?

Where should the retreat be held? The parish complex? A retreat facility? A rented hall? A campground?

Sometimes the Where? is driven by the When? You may choose to hold the retreat in May because that timing works best for your programming and for the target group. But when you check the date on the parish calendar, you find that the parish complex is reserved for a fund-raising auction. This event will also involve many of the parishioners who would volunteer to help you. You'll probably need to look at rearranging your schedule so that the retreat can be held at another time.

Cost can also affect where the retreat will be held. You may want to hold a day of reflection at a retreat facility to take advantage of the beauty of the setting and to create the feeling of moving away from everyday life. But the cost of renting the facility may be too much for your budget and for you to pass along to those attending.

In deciding where to hold the retreat, it's important to consider the nature of the retreat you have planned. For an overnight or weekend retreat, you'll need a facility that provides adequate sleeping quarters, showers, kitchen facilities, and recreational opportunities. That means the parish hall will not be the right setting for an overnight retreat, but it would be ideal for an afternoon family retreat.

The location for the retreat is an important part of the overall retreat experience. On the next page, there's a list of questions to help you decide Where?

General Questions

- Where is the facility? Will you need to provide maps or directions?
- Do any of the retreat participants have physical disabilities? If so, check with them to find out what accommodations they require. Will the facility be fully accessible for them?
- What is the cost? How and when does the facility require payment?
- How many and what size rooms are needed? Are these rooms available?
- Is there a separate chapel? Quiet space?
- Is there a room suitable for large-group work? Are there areas for small groups?
- How are the rooms furnished? What is the lighting like?
- Is there a place for indoor recreation? Outdoor recreation?
- Does more than one group use the facility at the same time? If so, how is time for the spaces scheduled?
- What equipment and supplies are available? What will you need to bring?
- Is there an indoor fireplace or an outdoor firepit?
- Does the facility provide snacks and meals?
- Can we choose to provide our own meals?
- What kind of cooking and dining facilities are available?
- Is there a refrigerator for storing soft drinks and snacks?
- In what areas of the facility are food and beverages allowed?
- Is there shopping nearby?
- Is there a pizza place nearby? Do they deliver?
- Are there extra charges for equipment, supplies, and materials used?
- Are there first-aid supplies available?
- Is there a hospital nearby?
- What are the retreat facility's rules? What will your group be responsible for?
- Does the facility have an on-site contact person?
- Does the facility require proof that your group is insured by your parish or diocese? (For information about this, check with the parish business manager or administrator.)
- How will the group get to the facility? How much will transportation cost?

Questions for Overnight Retreats

- How are the sleeping areas set up? What is the capacity?
- How are the areas separated for a coed group?
- What is provided for sleeping—beds, cots, bedding, pillows?
- Are towels provided?
- How many showers and sinks are available? Is this adequate? Or will you need to build extra time into the schedule so everyone will be able to use the showers?

Things to Keep in Mind

- Not all retreat facilities cater to youth and the ones that do are in demand. You may need to book a facility as much as a year before your retreat.
- The facility that sounds like a good thing over the telephone or looks good on a full-color brochure might be deceiving. It is always best to visit a facility before you book it. Call ahead to make sure someone will be around to let you in and show you around.
- Make sure you inquire about any extra costs—rental fee for the TV or VCR, charges for providing bed linens, towels.

HOW?

How? needs to be asked in every stage of your planning. Along with asking, Who is the target group? you'll want to ask, How will the target group learn about the retreat? How will it be publicized to them? When you ask, Who is needed to help? you'll also need to ask, How will volunteers be recruited?

Here are some other How? questions you'll want to consider.

- How can the parish be involved in the retreat?
  Ask parishioners to say prayers for a successful retreat and to write letters of affirmation to participants in the retreat. You may also need to ask parishioners for financial help.
- How can we involve the families of those attending the retreat?
  Provide parents with information about the retreat by sending them letters or by inviting them to a meeting. You may also ask parents and other family members for prayers and letters for retreat participants.
- How will we extend the benefits of the retreat beyond the initial experience?
  It is important for the retreat team to make plans not only for the retreat, but also for follow-up events and activities.
- How will we handle discipline?
  For suggestions for retreat guidelines, see Appendix page 94. Make sure you inform young people about any rules or guidelines that the retreat facility may have.
- How will the group get to the retreat facility?
  Can you ask parents to provide transportation? Will you need to rent a bus?
- How will it all come together?
  You will need to do your best with the planning and then place the retreat in God's hands. Remember, prayer is key to the success of a retreat.

The most important How? question is, How will the purpose and objectives of the retreat be accomplished? Your answer to that question will be the content of the retreat—the components you put together to create an effective retreat.

Five Focus Areas

The content of a retreat focuses on five areas:

1. Community Building
2. Message
3. Response
4. Prayer and Worship
5. Follow-up

Here are suggestions for covering these focus areas. Feel free to use and adapt these ideas to fit the needs of the target group and the skills and creativity of the retreat team.

In determining the content of a retreat, it is impossible to overestimate the importance of good planning. The quality of the retreat's content will reflect the quality of the preparation. For a checklist to use in your planning, see Appendix page 71.

FOCUS AREA #1—COMMUNITY BUILDING

Community building can happen in many ways throughout a retreat. Use community-building activities to:

- Help young people feel comfortable with one another at the beginning of the retreat. (You've no doubt heard of "icebreakers," but one of the young adult leaders I work with likes to call them "fire-starters.")
- Refocus the group after a break or meal.
- Set up the next activity.
- Teach a skill.

Community-building activities can be very simple, requiring no materials or setup, or very elaborate, requiring supplies, props, and time-consuming setup. The following list is to help you plan any activity, whether it is for community building or for another focus area.

Things to Keep in Mind

- Is the space suitable for the activity?
- Can everyone participate?
- Will this activity embarrass anyone or make anyone stand out in a negative way?
- Is the activity safe?
- Remember to **EXPLAIN** the activity, **DEMONSTRATE** what to do, and **ASK** if there are any questions. Be prepared to repeat your explanation if there are many questions.
- If the explanation of an activity takes longer then the actual activity, you may want to find a better way to explain it, simplify the activity, or choose another activity.

Community-Building Activities

Icebreakers

Use these activities to help group members get to know and feel comfortable with one another. You can also use icebreakers to energize a group and to help them learn to work as a team. Suggestions for icebreakers are included in the retreat models in this book, but you can also find one hundred icebreakers in *Getting Started: 100 Icebreakers for Youth Gatherings*. See Appendix page 96.

Songs

Use songs, ranging from silly to reflective, to:

- Reflect the theme of your retreat. A song that expresses the theme can be taught to the group early in the retreat and repeated at various times during the retreat.
- Emphasize a message that was shared.
- Introduce or serve as prayer. Worship songs can be upbeat and lively or reflective to fit the mood of the group.
- Break the ice, refocus the group, lead into an activity, or lighten the mood. Silly songs—from commercials, TV theme songs, camp songs, children's songs, movie soundtrack songs—fit these purposes perfectly.

Music Videos

Music videos of popular songs or music videos such as *VeggieTales* can be used as community builders. Just as with songs, you can use lighthearted music videos to change the mood, to help people to be comfortable with one another, to introduce an activity, or to present a message. If you are using a song to support the retreat's theme, you can use the music video of the song to reinforce its meaning.

Letters and Affirmations

There are many ways to use letters, notes, and written or spoken affirmations in building community. Letters and affirmations work best on a retreat in which the community has been gathered for a significant amount of time, such as an overnight or weekend retreat.

- "My Christ"

  I would like to explain this activity by telling you my own story about the first retreat that I experienced as a teen. We all put slips of paper with our names written on them into a bowl. Then each of us picked a name. Naturally, if you picked your own name, you put it back and picked again. You were not to tell anyone whose name you picked. You were to regard the person whose name you had selected as "My Christ." Throughout the retreat, you were to try to see Christ in this person and to be Christ for this person. The retreat leaders suggested nice things we could do—sit with the person at a meal or in large-group sessions, open a door, ask the person to join in a game, spend time with the person during a break. Later in the retreat, each of us wrote an affirmation letter to "My Christ." In our letters, we were encouraged to share how we saw Christ present in our "My Christ," what the retreat meant to us, what insights we were gaining from it, plus our hopes and prayers for our "My Christ." The letters were to be positive and uplifting, with no put-downs or snide remarks even if we knew our "My Christ" very well and were only kidding. Each of us sealed the affirmation letter in an envelope. The envelopes were collected and distributed during the final prayer service.

I still have my letter from that first retreat. It meant a lot to me at the time and still does today. Since then, I have used this activity many times and find that the experience can be powerful if teens approach it seriously.

Another option for picking "My Christ" names, particularly for retreats involving large numbers of participants, is for members of each small group to pick names within their own group.

"My Christ" letters can be distributed at the closing service of the retreat. I have also incorporated the exchange of "My Christ" letters into the closing Liturgy on a weekend retreat. In either case, set aside time for participants to talk about their retreat experiences. The retreat director begins the sharing and then calls on a team member. The team member shares and then calls on his or her "My Christ." The "My Christ" comes forward, receives his or her "My Christ" letter, shares retreat experiences, and calls on his or her own "My Christ." This process continues until all have shared.

If teens picked "My Christ" names within their small groups, the retreat director can call on small-group leaders to begin sharing. But whatever way you choose to distribute the "My Christ" letters, ask teens to wait until everyone has received a letter before they open and read their "My Christ" letters.

- Care Letters

Building community within families can happen even when all family members are not present for a retreat. To connect families with the retreat, ask parents or other family members to write letters to the participating teens. It usually takes some coordination to arrange parent/family letters, but the results are well worth the effort. I still cherish a letter I received from my mother during my first retreat. For a sample letter requesting and explaining parents/family letters, see Appendix page 87.

Although sharing parent/family letters with teens can be part of any retreat, it is probably best suited to weekend retreats and is frequently a part of Confirmation retreats.

These letters can be distributed in many different ways. The parent/family letters can be handed out after affirmations done in the small-group setting. Or distributing the letters can be part of a prayer service. Whatever way you choose to distribute the letters, it is important to allow participants time to read their letters privately. Plan to have tissues on hand because you will probably see some tears. Teens are often genuinely moved by what is said in these letters.

A word of caution: In all the years in which I have been involved in retreat ministry, either as a professional or as a volunteer, there have been only two incidents in which a participant received a negative letter from a parent. But you should have a plan in place in case it happens. You and the other adults who are helping you will want to be alert to anyone who may be having difficulty with what was written—positive or negative.

- Write-Back Option

To continue the retreat-to-home connection, encourage retreat participants to write letters back to their parent, parents, or family. Participants may want to hand-deliver these letters, or they may prefer to have you mail the letters.

- **Other Options for Letters of Affirmation**

  For a retreat or day of reflection for Confirmation candidates, consider asking sponsors to write encouraging letters to their candidates. I also like to invite family members other than parents to write letters. I do this in my letter to parents, encouraging them to ask other family members or friends to write letters to the participants. See the sample letter for parents, Appendix page 87.

  You may also wish to invite members of the church community—pastor, parish council members, staff members, senior citizens' group, and so on—to write to retreat participants.

  When there are affirmation letters for the participants from family members, parish members, and sponsors, I like to have participants receive the letters from their parents before the others so that their parents' letters stand out in their minds.

- **Affirmation Notes, or *Palanca***

  I first heard the word *palanca* on my first retreat. I still remember the explanation of the word. *Palanca* is a Spanish word meaning lever. A lever is used to lift or move something heavy. For our purposes, a palanca is a lever to help lift us spiritually or emotionally, to help us recognize the gifts we possess and the gift that each of us is.

  There are a variety of ways to do palancas, or affirmations.

  Palanca Bags

  Materials: A paper lunch bag or a medium-sized manila envelope for each person • small slips of paper • pens or pencils, one for each participant

  Preparation: Label each bag or envelope with a participant's name. Do this ahead of time, or have participants label their bags or envelopes.

  Directions: First explain palancas and give an example or two. Then explain that participants will be giving one another affirmations throughout the retreat. For very small groups, between ten and fifteen people, participants could write an affirmation for each person on the retreat. For larger groups, participants could write one affirmation for each person in their small group, including the group leader. After participants have written one palanca for each member in their small group, encourage them to write one for anyone else they would like to.

  Each affirmation should be addressed to the person for whom it is intended and must be signed by the writer. Affirmations are to be positive and uplifting. They are not to have a negative tone or include put-downs or snide remarks, even if participants know one another well and are only kidding. Affirmations can be written during breaks and free time and put into the bags or envelopes. Ask participants not to look in their own bags or envelopes. They will be given time to read palancas later in the retreat.

  Note: Check the bags or envelopes periodically to make sure that everyone is receiving affirmations.

- **Affirmation Papers**

  Materials: a 8 ½" by 11" sheet of paper and a pen or pencil for each person

  Directions: This activity works best for small groups. Have each participant write his or her name at the bottom of a sheet of paper and pass the sheet of paper to the person on his or her right. Participants are to write an affirmation for the person whose name is on the bottom of the paper they receive. Make sure participants know that what they write is to be positive and uplifting.

No put-downs or snide remarks are allowed, even if participants know one another well and are only kidding. The first person to receive a sheet of paper begins at the top of the sheet. After writing an affirmation, he or she folds the paper down to cover the affirmation and passes the paper to the right again. The next person writes his or her affirmation for the person at the "new" top, directly below the fold. The process continues until the papers return to their original owners.

Variation: Give group members one slip of paper for each person in the small group. Have participants label each slip of paper with the name of a person in their small group and write an affirmation on each slip. These slips of paper can then be given to the person they are intended for.

After each person has received his or her own sheet of paper or slips of paper, allow time for participants to read the affirmations they have received, either out loud to the group or to themselves.

- Verbal Affirmations

We seldom hear verbal affirmations of others or of ourselves. Far too often, we hear the quick criticism, put-down, snide remark, or negative comment.

Verbal affirmation is a skill we need to learn. It should become commonplace in our conversations with and about others. So it's important for us to practice affirmations.

- Affirmation Circles

This activity works best in small groups and probably at the end of the retreat, after participants have had a chance to get to know and feel comfortable with one another.

Introduce the activity in the large-group setting. Explain the need for verbal affirmation. Point out that in giving affirmations, it is important to speak directly to the person being affirmed, to use the first person ("I"), and to be specific. It is equally important for the person being affirmed to accept the affirmation without commenting on it in any way, except to say "Thank you."

Give real examples of how to affirm someone verbally. For example, the retreat director may affirm members of the retreat team. The persons affirmed can provide examples of how to respond.

To practice verbal affirmations, ask teens to join their small groups. Have each group sit in a circle on chairs or the floor.

Option 1

Assign one person to the "hot seat," the middle of the circle. This person moves around the circle, facing one person at a time. The person in the circle affirms the person in the hot seat. Each member of the group, including the small-group leader, takes a turn in the hot seat.

Option 2

Provide a small lighted candle for each group. Hand the candle to one person and ask the rest of the group to affirm that person. When this person has received a verbal affirmation from each member of the group, he or she passes the candle to the next person. The process continues until each person has been affirmed.

Option 3

Have participants write affirmations on slips of paper, one slip for each person in the group. Participants can take turns verbalizing and distributing each affirmation to the person for whom it was written. This is a good way for a group that has a hard time being spontaneous to do verbal affirmations.

Free Time and Breaks

These terms, *free time* and *breaks*, are sometimes used interchangeably. Both free time and breaks are planned time to allow for a break from the regular schedule. Both provide opportunities for participants to unwind, relax, and to build community in an informal manner. Free time is generally a longer period of a more unstructured nature.

In building free time and breaks into a retreat, you need to find the right balance. Too much free time can break the flow of the retreat. But if teens are given too little free time, they may become distracted and misbehave. A good rule of thumb to follow is that the longer the retreat, the more free time and breaks need to be scheduled.

Organized Free Time and Breaks

- Snack Breaks
  Fifteen- to thirty-minute breaks for drinks and snacks.

- Activity Breaks
  Fifteen- to thirty-minute breaks for a change of pace: noncompetitive games, structured outdoor or gym time, competitive games between small groups—board games, card games not connected to gambling, friendly games of volleyball, basketball, and so on.

Nonorganized Free Time and Breaks

- After-Meal Breaks
  Fifteen- to thirty-minute breaks to allow time to freshen up, do after-meal clean-up, and take restroom breaks.

- Free Time
  Thirty-minute to two-hour breaks to nap, go to the gym, play games, watch a movie, have a snack.

Note: For free time or breaks, be sure to list options for activities and give guidelines as needed. During a weekend retreat, allow for a longer period of free time on Saturday. Weather and facility permitting, encourage teens to spend some time outside.

Announcements

It is important to provide basic information before sending participants into an activity or break. Announcements should be short, to the point, and made at appropriate times. For example, at the beginning of the meal, you might need to announce that no one is to leave the dining area until announcements are made. Then, at the end of the meal, you can announce what time participants are to meet and where, what group is responsible for meal clean-up, and options for activities.

Note: Sometimes it helps to have the participants repeat the meeting time to you before they leave for their break.

FOCUS AREA #2—MESSAGE

The message is the heart of the retreat. Because we all learn in different ways and at different paces, use a variety of methods to present the message. Make use of presentations, activities, dramas, skits, listening, singing, discussing, observing, writing, and other creative approaches of your own.

Things to Keep in Mind

- Use the length of the retreat to determine the number and variety of methods to include. Be realistic. Resist the urge to add activities just because they are good or enriching.
- Focus on the message. Make sure the message remains consistent when you combine different methods.
- Activities provide experiences that lead to understanding. Quiet activities provide time for participants to reflect on what they are learning, time to be with God, and an atmosphere that encourages all to share.

Methods

Presentations

Use brief structured talks to convey specific information on a particular topic. Any qualified member of the retreat team can give these presentations.

Witness Talks

Witness talks, usually between fifteen and thirty minutes long, support factual presentations with personal stories of faith. Anyone involved in the retreat may be invited to prepare and give a witness talk. Encourage teens to participate. For suggestions on preparing witness talks, see Appendix page 74.

Things to Keep in Mind

- Presentations and witness talks should have a scriptural focus. Select at least one passage from Scripture that connects with the retreat's message or is the basis of the message. This passage should be read and referred to during presentations and witness talks.
- Speaking in the first person ("I") will keep presentations and witness talks from becoming preachy.
- Presentations should include examples of firsthand personal experience. People listen more carefully when we share our own stories with them. These stories should fit the theme of the presentation or witness talk, and they should be true. To use a popular expression, teens can "spot a phony a mile away."

Things to Keep in Mind —continued

- It is a good idea to have the retreat director and/or retreat team review the presentations and witness talks that will be given during the retreat. This can be done as part of the preparation for the retreat. This review can help you make sure that what is being shared is well prepared and in line with current teachings and practices of the Church, and can also help you to write reflection questions for the presentations.

Film and Video

Use these effective teaching tools to:

- Introduce the theme of the retreat.
- Enhance a talk or teaching.
- Emphasize a point.

Panel of Speakers

Invite a panel of speakers to share their lived experience on the retreat theme. The speakers can present information or personal testimony or take questions from retreat participants. This approach can challenge and broaden participants' views.

Skits

Having participants create skits, dramas, role-playing situations, and radio and television commercials can deepen learning, support the retreat theme, build community, set the mood for another activity, or provide an outlet for energy or a means of entertainment.

Things to Keep in Mind

- Establish guidelines. Warn groups not to use suggestive or offensive language or themes, and not to do take-offs on movies or TV shows that use suggestive or offensive language or themes.
- Set a reasonable limit for preparation time, probably no more than fifteen minutes.
- Set a reasonable time limit for the skits or other presentations, probably from one to five minutes, but no more than five minutes.

Stories

Use stories to:

- Introduce a retreat theme or activity.
- Emphasize a point.
- Make connections between the retreat theme and lived experience.

- Convey a message.
- Set a mood.

Sources for stories include:

- Poems
- Songs
- Stories from real life
- Stories written by teens
- Fiction
- Children's stories
- Stories from magazines and newspapers

You'll find twenty-five stories, complete with questions for reflection and journaling, in *Making Connections: 25 Stories for Sharing Faith with Teens*. See Appendix page 96.

Sending Forth

At the end of a retreat, it is important to wrap up the experience for the teens and to "send them forth." This wrap-up serves to:

- Summarize the message of the retreat.
- Challenge participants to act on the retreat message.
- Help participants to own the experience and grow from it.

This can be done by creating a ritual or activity with the sending forth in mind or by asking participants to take turns sharing their reactions to the retreat.

FOCUS AREA #3—RESPONSE

Offering activities to help participants respond to the message of the retreat helps to deepen the message in their hearts. This also gives teens the opportunity to begin thinking of ways to make practical changes in their lives. Giving teens the message "Just say 'No'" to deal with the issue of premarital sex doesn't help them to develop the skill to do so. The message would be much more effective if it were supported by exercises to help teens gain the necessary skills to put the message into practice in their lives.

Here are examples of activities to help teens respond to a message.

Reflection Questions

Reflection questions are a good tool to help young people focus on and relate a message to their own lives. The most effective reflection questions are open-ended and prepared ahead of time.

Use reflection questions:

- after a presentation or witness talk.
- before a topic is to be discussed.
- in conjunction with a video or portion of a video.
- to stimulate small-group discussion.

Journaling

Journaling is a good way for young people to create a record of their responses. If you plan to include journaling in the retreat schedule, be sure to provide notebooks. If the budget will allow it, provide attractive notebooks that teens will find appealing and that they will want to keep. I find it works well to give teens time for journaling after a presentation or witness talk, just before they go into their small groups for discussion. Provide reflection questions and ask teens to respond to these questions in their journals.

You may want to use a journaling activity to open a weekend retreat. Give each participant a journal or notebook. Ask each to write the name and date of the retreat on the first page. For the first journal entry, ask each teen to write about the gift he or she would like to receive from the Lord by the end of the retreat—a better self-image, a deeper assurance of God's love, and so on. Then ask teens to journal about how they need to cooperate with the Lord in order to receive this gift. Before they begin writing, point out that they will need to be open to and involved in the retreat experience.

When leading a retreat, I like to share with teens these thoughts, which I heard on my first retreat: A retreat isn't something that is done to you, it is something that involves you. What you put into a retreat is what you get out of it.

Be sure to ask teens to review this journal entry at the end of the retreat to evaluate how open they allowed themselves to be to the retreat and to the possibility of receiving the gifts they want. Be sensitive to the fact that, at the end of the retreat, teens may or may not feel that they have received these gifts. You may need to point out that the Lord may still be giving their gifts to them. They may need to continue to be open to receiving the gifts, in the Lord's time and in the Lord's way.

Letters to Jesus

Ask young people to write letters to Jesus about the areas of their lives that were addressed by a presentation or activity. Consider giving teens an opening line to help them get started. After a presentation or activity on self-image, you may ask teens to begin their letters to Jesus with this or a similar sentence:

Dear Jesus,

When I look at myself in a mirror, what I see is....

Writing letters to Jesus can also be part of a reconciliation service. Teens can focus on telling Jesus about the ways in which they have sinned and asking him for forgiveness.

Note: Writing these letters in a reconciliation service should never take the place of or be seen as equivalent to celebrating the sacrament of Penance.

Large-Group Sharing

Some retreat themes and presentations lend themselves to large-group sharing. Successful large-group sharing requires advance preparation. Prepare open-ended questions that will challenge the young people to be candid. Encourage all to participate.

Another way to prepare for large-group discussion is to have young people write and turn in questions anonymously. This can free young people to ask questions without fear of embarrassment. You will want to read the questions before you use them with the group. Because the questions are anonymous, some young people may write questions with some shock value.

For large-group sharing on sensitive topics, such as sexuality or relationships, have participants form two same-sex groups. Ask each group to write their questions and put them into a box for separate discussions.

Before using the questions for large-group sharing, sort them into topic areas. I usually make copies of the questions for members of the retreat team. Then during a break, the team meets to review the questions. We discuss questions that we feel we might have trouble answering. If we can, we try to find answers for these questions. If there are questions that we can't answer, we admit that to the group. We volunteer to find the answers after the retreat and invite teens to contact us later.

Small-Group Sharing

Small groups can provide an atmosphere that encourages teens to share their thoughts, feelings, and experiences about the main messages of the retreat.

For successful small-group sharing, form the groups at the beginning of the retreat. Try to split friendship groups to encourage teens to get to know other participants. Allow teens and leaders to remain in the same small groups for the duration of the retreat. Ideally, small groups should have a minimum of five members and a maximum of nine members, with competent and caring adults or young adults serving as leaders. Ideally, these leaders should be trained in directing small groups. It is also very beneficial to have trained peer leaders serve as co-leaders. Small-group leaders should participate as well as lead the groups.

Small groups are effective in processing the message of the retreat. The most important questions involved in the message will probably be handled in small groups. Prepare open-ended questions that will challenge the young people.

Begin with an introductory small-group activity to build community and trust and to help participants and leaders get to know one another.

Things to Keep in Mind

- Introduce the retreat director and retreat team members.
- Establish the small-group leaders' authority.
- Make sure everyone is comfortable. Group members should be seated on the same level, either on chairs or on the floor, able to make eye contact with one another. Make sure no one is sitting outside of the group.
- Encourage all—leaders and participants—to relax and be themselves.
- Set guidelines for sharing, ideally allowing participants to suggest at least some of these. For example, anything shared in the small group is not to be repeated outside that group, unless permission is given to do so.
- Encourage all members of the group to make a commitment to following the guidelines. You may even want to have group members sign simple contracts, promising to observe these guidelines.
- Leaders need to stimulate discussion and invite everyone to participate without dominating the discussion.
- Leaders should be as open to sharing as they are encouraging members of their group to be.
- Always open and close the small-group sharing with prayer. Encourage group members to take turns offering simple spontaneous prayers.

Note: If, during small-group sharing, a group leader becomes aware that a teen is dealing with a harmful or potentially harmful situation, the leader needs to handle the information in a responsible manner that respects confidentiality. The group leader will probably want to speak privately with the teen to verify the information, but should not promise to keep secret the situation or the identity of the teen involved. In fact, the group leader is responsible for making sure that there is an appropriate follow-up. He or she should encourage the teen to talk to the retreat director. If the retreat director is not the parish contact for the retreat group, then the retreat director is responsible for finding the proper contact and making sure that appropriate action is taken to protect the teen and provide help.

Personal Prayer Time

I see a great benefit in providing time for personal prayer, especially on a weekend retreat. Personal prayer can take many forms and be either directed or undirected. It is helpful to give a brief presentation on prayer and to suggest prayer options the teens could try. For prayer options, see Appendix pages 76 and 81.

Emmaus Walk

Luke 24:13-35 is the scriptural basis for this activity. In this passage, two men are walking on the road to Emmaus, talking about the death of Jesus when the resurrected Christ joins them and they fail to recognize him.

Have the young people pair up, and give each pair a question designed to help them share with each other how the message of a presentation applies to them. Before sending the pairs off on an actual walk, give them guidelines for where to walk and how to share. For example, for ten minutes, one person interviews and the other person answers the question. Then when they turn around and walk back, the partners switch roles. Before the pairs begin their walk, offer a brief prayer asking Christ to walk with them as he did with the two men on the road to Emmaus.

Dramas and Skits

Use dramas and skits to help teens respond to a message. Here's an example of how a skit can support other methods of responding to the message.

Theme of Retreat: Unity in the Body of Christ

Presentation: Based on 1 Corinthians 12.

Response: Silent reflection and journaling on reflection questions based on the presentation

Response: Small-group discussion of the reflection questions

Response: Small groups work to create skits on unity. Each group can take a different focus on unity—school, family, friendship group, community, Church community.

Hands-on Activities

Participating in hands-on activities can help teens gain insights into themselves and share these insights with those around them.

When you're considering using a hands-on activity, ask:

- Is the activity just keeping us busy, or is it helping to deepen the message within us?
- Is the space available conducive to doing this activity?
- Are the materials readily available?
- Will there be a cost involved in doing this activity? If so, do we have the financial resources to cover the cost?

Here are suggestions for hands-on activities.

- Draw it. (Draw an image that depicts the retreat message for you.)
- Mold it. (Make a symbol of the retreat message out of modeling clay.)
- Write it. (Write a poem, prayer, personal creed, or story that expresses the message for you.)

FOCUS AREA #4—PRAYER AND WORSHIP

Prayer and worship are significant parts of any retreat experience. Opportunities for prayer and worship help to build community within the group, and participants' personal contributions bring a sense of ownership to prayer experiences. Prayer can be as simple as a meal prayer, taking time to thank God for food as nourishment and to acknowledge food as a blessing. Prayer can be more elaborate, involving, for example, a reconciliation service. Some prayer experiences may need to be prepared well in advance, as with a reconciliation service. Other prayer and prayer experiences can be prepared by participants during the retreat. Participants, either as individuals or in groups, can be responsible for meal prayers and portions of prayer services or Liturgies.

Use these questions to guide your planning of prayer and worship experiences for a retreat.

- What prayer experiences do we want or need to have?
- Whom do we need to make this happen? (If the retreat team wants to include a reconciliation service that involves celebrating the sacrament of Penance or if the team wants the retreat group to celebrate a Liturgy, the team will need to make sure that a priest will be available.)
- Have we contacted and scheduled all the people we will need to help us?
- What materials and supplies will we need for our prayer experiences?
- Are we using music in an order of worship? (If so, the team will need to request copyright permission or contact the parish liturgist to see whether the parish has contracts with music publishers that will allow reprinting music.)

Here are some suggestions for prayer experiences for retreats.

Meditation and Journey Prayer

This type of prayer experience requires that participants relax their bodies, close their eyes, and use their imaginations to take a journey through prayer. The journey will help participants look at various questions and situations in their lives. In most prayer journeys, participants meet Jesus, who speaks to them, asks them questions, or has them think about issues. Participants imagine how they would respond to Jesus.

When the meditation or prayer journey is over, participants process their experience. I find it beneficial to have them journal about their experience before they discuss it. If you choose to ask participants to do this, have journaling questions posted where everyone can see them.

Many resources provide meditations and journey prayers, including *Paths of Prayer: A Textbook of Prayer and Meditation*. See Appendix page 96.

PRAYERS AND BLESSINGS

Opening Prayer

A retreat usually opens with a prayer or prayer service that includes a clear statement of the theme and Scripture readings that support the theme. Within the opening prayer, you may want to ask for a blessing upon all who are gathered for the retreat.

Closing Prayer

Close the retreat with a prayer or prayer service that reviews the theme of the retreat, repeats the supporting Scripture, and summarizes the message of the retreat. Send all forth with a blessing.

Prayer Before a Presentation

Begin presentations by asking all to join you in prayer for the person who is speaking and for those who are listening.

Prayers for the Retreat Team

As the team meets to plan the retreat and before the retreat begins, gather the retreat team for prayer. Schedule time for the team to pray together during a weekend or overnight retreat.

Small-Group Prayer

Encourage small groups to open and close with a prayer each time they meet.

Meal Prayers

Ask for volunteers to lead meal prayers. Team members can work with the volunteers to make them feel more comfortable. Encourage teens to use "fun" prayers they may have learned at summer camp or at youth ministry gatherings.

PRAYER SERVICES

On overnight or weekend retreats, begin and close each day with community prayer times. You will probably want to include music, activities, and Scripture.

Here's an example of a format for morning prayer that includes community building, movement to wake people up, and direction for moving into the next activity.

- To get teens to move out of their friendship groups, begin with an icebreaker game such as "Back-to-Back, People-to-People" from *Getting Started: 100 Icebreakers for Youth Gatherings*. See Appendix page 96.
- After a minute or two, ask the partners to do a "mirror activity." Suggest an activity to be acted out; peeling a banana, for example. Then have one partner act out the activity while the other partner, as the mirror reflection, tries to repeat what his or her partner is doing as exactly as possible. Give both partners a chance to be the mirror reflection.
- Ask partners to sit facing each other, closing their eyes, and holding each other's hands. Each partner prays silently for his or her partner, who accepts the prayer.
- Include a Scripture reading that fits with the activities of the upcoming day.
- The retreat director or a member of the retreat team closes by praying out loud for the goals of the day.

Here's an example of an evening prayer that relaxes and quiets people. By having people praying for one another, they are also building community.

The Living Rosary

- Ask the group to sit in a circle.
- Have members of the retreat team take turns leading the decades of the rosary.
- The leader begins the decade with the Our Father. Teens pass a candle to symbolize Christ's presence. The candle is passed before each Hail Mary. The person who has received the candle asks the group to pray for a specific intention, prays the Hail Mary, and passes the candle. The leader closes the decade with the Glory Be to the Father.
- The leader of the next decade begins with the Our Father, and the process is repeated.
- If there are fewer than fifty people in the group, each person may receive the candle twice. If there are more than fifty people in the group, each person should still receive the candle once and have a chance to voice a prayer intention.

Scripture

Provide opportunities for young people to enter into Scripture by studying it, praying with it, and reflecting on it.

Use these questions to guide your use of Scripture.

- Will this be a small-group or large-group activity?
- What Scripture will we use?
- Will you begin or follow up with a presentation on the Scripture?
- After teens have prayed and reflected on the Scripture, do you want them to share with partners? In their small groups? In the large group?

Here's an example of an activity that encourages teens to work with Scripture. For a reproducible handout for teens, see Appendix page 76.

Stirring of the Spirit

- Begin with a brief prayer, asking the Holy Spirit to guide the group in reflecting on what the Lord is telling us in the Scripture.
- Read or have a volunteer read the Scripture passage.
- Reread the passage slowly. Ask teens to imagine that they are present at the scene in which the Scripture takes place.
- Allow a minute or two for teens to reflect on what is said and done in the Scripture.
- Ask teens to journal their responses to these questions.
  What is the image of God I see in this passage?
  With what person or event do I identify most in this passage?
  In this passage, what do I feel the Lord is telling me?

Liturgical Prayer

In preparing liturgical prayer, give attention to the norms and guidelines established for their celebration. When planning a Mass or a reconciliation service that includes celebration of the sacrament of Penance, it is helpful if the priest is involved in the planning or is at least aware and accepting of what is planned.

- Reconciliation and Healing Services

  Because the purpose of reconciliation and healing services is to allow Christ's love to free people from the barriers and burdens they bring to the retreat, these services are appropriate to any retreat, no matter what the theme.

- Eucharistic Liturgy

  Celebrating Mass together can be a memorable experience for a group gathered for a retreat. The retreat team can plan the Mass before or during the retreat. If you decide to plan the Mass during the retreat, you can involve everyone in the planning. The small groups can take responsibility for different areas of the planning: music, environment, writing prayers of the faithful, writing prayers of thanksgiving, preparing and doing the readings, preparing and distributing an order of worship. You will need to consult with the priest during the planning.

FOCUS AREA #5—FOLLOW-UP

A retreat is just a beginning, the place for new growth to start. This growth needs to be encouraged. To keep a retreat from becoming an isolated event, plan follow-up activities and events as you plan the retreat. Integrate these activities into the existing parish youth ministry programming or the high school campus ministry plan.

Evaluations

Requiring participants—both team members and teens—to do an evaluation provides a way to determine whether the purpose and objectives of the retreat have been accomplished. Honest evaluations will enable planners to enhance the next retreat experience. For a sample of an evaluation, see Appendix page 85.

Things to Keep in Mind

- The most beneficial evaluations are written and anonymous. In general, anonymity allows for honest responses. Be aware, however, that anonymity also allows some teens to take an immature approach to the evaluations.
- Some negative comments will need to be taken with a grain of salt, but negative comments should not be ignored.
- The value of conflicting comments will need to weighed by retreat team members. For example, one teen may think there was too little free time given. Another teen may think there was too much free time. The retreat team should be able to set these two comments into perspective.
- Receiving one or two negative evaluations does not mean the retreat was not effective.

Here are suggestions for other follow-up activities.

Letters

Near the end of the retreat, have young people write letters to themselves. Ask them to include their thoughts about what they are taking with them from the experience—what they want to remember, how have they grown, how they experienced God, and other thoughts they want to include. Assure them that no one will see their letters. When everyone has had a chance to finish writing, provide envelopes for their letters. Ask teens to address the envelopes to themselves and seal them. Collect the envelopes and tell teens that you will mail their letters to them in about four months.

Follow-up Letters

About two months after the retreat, send letters to those who participated. Personalize the letters if you can. Include stories of things that happened on the retreat and copies of the group picture if one was taken.

Restating the theme of the retreat may help to remind participants of the challenges presented during the retreat and the growth they experienced. It would be ideal if these letters could also serve as invitations to or reminders of a follow-up event. The letters could be sent via snail mail or e-mail.

Follow-up Activities

- Pizza Party

  Have a gathering a few weeks after the retreat to provide an opportunity for participants to socialize and for you to announce the schedule of follow-up activities.

- Bible Study and Faith-Sharing Groups

  Offer teens the chance to participate in Bible study or faith-sharing groups. You will want to plan for these groups while you are planning the retreat so that you can announce tentative schedules and topics at the end of the retreat. To help you create programs that will be meaningful to teens, include questions about teens' interests and scheduling preferences on the retreat evaluations.

- Day of Recollection

  As you are planning the retreat, plan a day of recollection to follow-up on the retreat. Announce this event at the end of retreat.

- Youth Group

  If there is an active youth group in your parish, invite members of the retreat group to participate. If there is no youth group, invite retreat participants to meet after the retreat to make plans for beginning a youth group.

- Catechetical Programs

  If the retreat is part of your catechetical programming, consider how can you build on it or follow it up. If interest in a particular topic surfaced on the evaluations, consider addressing that topic in future catechetical programming.

- Discipleship Opportunities

  Consider ways to offer peer ministry training to those who have participated in the retreat. The youth ministry department of your diocese may be able to offer advice or may already have established peer ministry and leadership training. Or you may be able to join with neighboring parishes to provide this training. Young people who receive this important training can become part of future retreat teams and also can be instrumental in establishing or strengthening meaningful activities for youth within the parish.

Recruiting Adult and Teen Volunteers

Before you begin asking for help, decide what roles you need to fill and what tasks go along with each role. The following task lists can guide your planning.

Retreat Coordinator and/or Director

This role can be handled by one person or shared by two people. Because some of these tasks may already be part of their jobs, the parish youth minister or high school campus minister may also be the retreat coordinator or director.

Tasks Prior to the Retreat

- Is responsible for the overall retreat design and implementation
- Recruits and supervises the retreat team
- Develops timeline and agenda for retreat team meetings
- Calls for, schedules, and runs team meetings
- Makes sure all tasks are assigned and accomplished
- Develops all correspondence—letters to parents and participants, permission forms, medical releases, and so on
- Makes sure that all necessary permissions have been received from participants
- Secures facility for the retreat
- Develops and handles retreat budget, including record-keeping, deposits, check requests, making payments
- Determines method of transportation and arranges for travel
- Determines what meals and snacks need to be provided, based on the retreat format and facility chosen
- Determines what supplies will be needed and makes sure they are available
- Prays for the retreat team, participants, and the success of the retreat

Tasks During the Retreat

- Directs and implements the retreat schedule
- Directs team meetings during overnight and weekend retreats
- Functions as a presenter
- Enforces rules and discipline
- Sets up all supplies necessary for presentations and activities

Spiritual Director

The person who takes on this role does not necessarily have to be an ordained minister.

Tasks Prior to the Retreat

- Provides spiritual direction for the retreat team
- Attends team meetings as necessary
- Leads and/or delegates leaders for worship and prayer times for team meetings
- Helps in planning prayer and worship experiences for the retreat
- Arranges for clergy needed for the retreat
- Secures all supplies needed for prayer and worship experiences
- Prays for the retreat team, participants, and the success of the retreat

Tasks During the Retreat

- Directs, or delegates the responsibility for directing, worship and prayer times
- Sets up all supplies necessary for prayer experiences
- Helps enforce rules and discipline

Small-Group Leaders

Tasks Prior to the Retreat

- Attend team meetings
- Help in planning the retreat
- Pray for the retreat team, participants, and the success of the retreat

Tasks During the Retreat

- Facilitate small groups
- Help create or select and lead icebreakers and other community-building activities
- Function as presenters and/or give witness talks as determined by the retreat team
- Act as adult chaperones in a dorm
- Help chaperone free-time activities
- Help enforce rules and discipline

Peer Leaders

Tasks Prior to the Retreat

- Attend team meetings
- Help in planning the retreat
- Pray for the retreat team, participants, and the success of the retreat

Tasks During the Retreat

- Help in small groups as facilitators or co-facilitators
- Help create or select and lead icebreakers and other community-building activities
- Function as presenters and/or give witness talks as determined by the retreat team
- Provide leadership and positive role models
- Serve as peer listeners
- Help enforce rules and discipline

Food Coordinator

This person assumes responsibility for all the meals and snacks needed for the retreat.

Tasks Prior to the Retreat

- Attends retreat team meetings as necessary
- Plans meals and snacks
- Works with the retreat coordinator and/or director to schedule meals and snacks
- Secures budget information from the director/coordinator
- Checks with retreat facility on availability of equipment and supplies
- Checks with retreat director and/or coordinator about special dietary needs or food allergies of participants
- Plans menus
- Secures all necessary food and supplies
- Makes arrangements for food preparations, including recruiting volunteers to help
- Prays for the retreat team, participants, and the success of the retreat

Tasks During the Retreat

- Directs preparation of meals and snacks
- Sets up all the necessary supplies
- Acts as an adult chaperone in a dorm
- Helps enforce rules and discipline

Other Roles*

- Leaders of prayer and worship
- Photographer
- Clerical support
- Music and song leaders
- Dorm chaperones

*Some of these roles can be combined. For instance, a small-group leader may also serve as photographer or song leader. A word of caution—make sure that no one person takes on so many roles that he or she becomes ineffective in any of them.

HOW TO RECRUIT VOLUNTEERS

Choose volunteers who are effective and comfortable working with the age group of the retreat participants. Look for people who have an active faith life of their own and a sense of humor. The ideal volunteers will be open-minded, understanding, compassionate, and good listeners.

Screen potential volunteers.
- Find out where volunteers' gifts and talents are.
- Check on their availability for planning.
- Find out what experience they have.
- Find out what need for training they may have.
- Ask why they want to help.
- Do a background check with the local police department.

Where to Find Volunteers?

For adult volunteers, consider:
- Volunteers in past youth ministry programs
- Recommendations from the parish staff and from young people
- Stewardship forms that list time and talents
- Parishioners who are teachers
- Those who have participated in the parish adult retreats and adult religious education programs, such as Bible study
- Members of small faith communities within your parish

For young adult volunteers, consider:
- Those who have attended retreats or participated in other youth ministry programs
- Recommendations of area high school and college campus ministers
- Members of the parish young adult group
- Those who have participated in adult religious education programs, such as Bible study
- Recommendations of the parish staff

For peer leaders, consider:
- Those who have recently been confirmed
- Those who have already attended a retreat
- Recommendations from other young people, from area high school campus ministers, and from parish staff

I have not found bulletin announcements effective in recruiting volunteers. When I have put together a list of potential volunteers, I usually begin the recruitment process by sending each person a letter. In the letter I explain that the person has either been recommended to me or that I have noticed something about the person that I consider important for working with young people. I clearly state what role I am asking the person to consider, what is expected, and how much time is likely to be involved. I also enclose a description of the role and a list of its tasks. With the letter, I enclose a self-addressed stamped envelope with a response form to return by a specific date. The response form can include these options:

❑ Yes, I would love to be a part of the retreat team.
❑ No, I can't commit to being part of the retreat team at this time, but contact me again.
❑ Sorry, but I'm not interested.

Please list people you feel might be interested in helping on this retreat, along with some qualities that make these people good candidates for the retreat team.

_____

_____

_____

The next step is to follow up with phone calls to everyone who has received a letter. Personal contact is very important!

Who's in the House?

Theme: Celebrating Family

Scripture Focus: Romans 8:15-17

Target Group: Middle school and/or high school teens, along with their families. The retreat can also include all members of the family, as long as appropriate activities are planned for the younger children.

Purpose: To have families take time out of their normal routines to strengthen family relationships, communication, and prayer.

Objectives: To help family members to • better understand the meaning of family • take time to share together • have an opportunity to pray together

Materials: Nametags • markers • large sheets of drawing paper • sheets of writing paper • pens or pencils and index cards, one for each participant • a whistle or bell or some other device to call time • snacks • soft drinks • napkins • paper cups

Preparations: Arrange for an area for the large-group presentation, areas or rooms for small groups, a place to serve snacks, and a place to have prayer. If possible, arrange to use the church for prayer. If you are providing childcare for children younger than kindergarten age, you will also need a room for a nursery.

If you are inviting all the members of the family to participate, you will need to have retreat team members to work with the age groups outlined here.

> **· Pre-kindergarten Age**

It would be ideal to provide a nursery for young children. Have games and toys, storybooks, and, if possible, some appropriate videos. This area should be close to a bathroom.

Children who are older than three can do some drawing activities about family and share their feelings about family with a retreat team member. They can also join their families for family prayer time and for snacks and drinks.

Try to have team members of both sexes working with this age group.

> **· Kindergartners through second-graders**

This age group can meet during the presentation and small-group time. Team members can spend some time playing games with this group and talking about what a family is and why family is important. Children can draw pictures of their families at the table, showing their favorite things to eat and drink and perhaps a favorite game that they play at the table. Team members will need to limit the number of things children are to draw on the table. Children can also draw pictures of their favorite places in their homes. When everyone has finished drawing, children can take turns sharing and explaining their drawings. Team members can encourage children to talk about how we are all members of the family of God. Children should be affirmed for their work. Before they join their families for the break, the group can close with a song about family, such as "We Are a Family" by Larry Folk, from the cassette *We Are a Family*, Oregon Catholic Press, 800-548-8749. Or use a song from *VeggieTales*.

> ### • Third- through sixth-graders

This age group can meet during the presentation and small-group time. It would be best to form groups of third- and fourth-graders and groups of fifth- and sixth-graders. Team members can spend some time playing a few games and then talk with children about what a family is and why family is important. Young people can draw pictures of their families at the table, with their favorite meals and snacks on the table. They can also write their favorite family activities and the things they think are important for families to talk about. Team members will need to limit how many things young people can draw on the table and how many things they can write. When everyone has finished, young people can take turns sharing and explaining their drawings.

On the back of their drawings, young people can draw or write what it means to them to be members of the family of God. Young people should be encouraged to talk about what they have drawn or written. Team members can share a modified version of the presentation, pages 37-39, and ask these young people to share their reactions. Team members can share one or two appropriate Scripture passages with this group: Romans 8:15-17, Galatians 3:26-29, Ephesians 4:2-6. Young people should be affirmed for their work and join their families for the break.

> ### • Seventh- and eighth-graders
> ### • Ninth- and tenth-graders
> ### • Eleventh- and twelfth-graders
> ### • Adults

These age groups can remain together for large-group activities. For the small-group activities, each age group can form one or more small groups. Small groups are most effective when there are fewer than ten members in each group. A team member should be available to work with each of these groups.

Adult small groups do not necessarily need team members to act as facilitators. They can form their own small groups and be given directions about what to share within their groups.

7:00 pm

Arrival and Welcome

As participants arrive, ask them to fill out and wear nametags. Make sure members of the retreat team are available to meet and greet families and to show them where to go.

Note: If you are providing childcare, ask parents to okay the snack their children will be having and provide any information caregivers will need to know about their children.

7:10 pm

Opening

Introduce the retreat director and the retreat team. Present the theme and objectives of the retreat and provide a brief overview of the evening.

Community-Building Activity

Option 1

Ask parents and kids to gather in family units. Tell them that they will be given different topics to share with their families. When they hear the whistle, or whatever device you use to get their attention, the person who is speaking needs to finish his or her sentence quickly so that the family can move to the next topic. Pick four or five topics. Here are some suggestions.

- What cartoon, TV show, song, or movie makes you think of your own family? Why?
- What is your favorite room in your home? Why?
- What is your favorite family memory? Why?
- What was the best vacation your family ever took? Why?
- (For the kids) What one family rule would you like to change? Why?
- (For the adults) What family rule did I want to change when I was a teenager? Why?
- The biggest challenge I face right now is….
- A wish I have for my family is that….

Option 2

Hand out index cards and pens or pencils, one for each family member. Ask members of the family to pair off, with partners sitting back to back. It's best to have each parent pair off with a child. Then give these directions. Display a large sample of an index card with the appropriate markings.

- Draw a line down the center of your index card.
- At the top of the left half of the card, write your partner's name.
- Along the left side of the card, going down, write the numbers 1-7.
- At the top of the right half of the card, write "me."
- Along the right side of the center line, going down, write the numbers 1-7.

my partner	me
1.	1.
2.	2.
3.	3.
4.	4.
5.	5.
6.	6.
7.	7.

Ask participants not to look at their partners during this exercise. Then explain that you are going to ask them questions about their partners. They are to write answers to these questions on the left side of their cards. They are to answer the questions for themselves on the right side of the card. Make sure that all participants understand the directions before you continue with these or similar questions.

1. What shoes is your partner wearing today? (What shoes are you wearing today?)
2. What color are your partner's eyes? (What color are your eyes?)
3. What color shirt is your partner wearing today? (What color shirt are you wearing today?)
4. What is your partner's favorite TV show? (What is your favorite TV show?)
5. What is your partner's favorite place in the house? (What is your favorite place in the house?)
6. What kind of music does your partner like to listen to? (What kind of music do you like to listen to?)
7. What is your partner's favorite pastime? (What is your favorite pastime?)

When everyone has written answers for all the questions, have partners turn around, face one another, and share their responses without making critical comments about incorrect answers. Urge them to have fun with the sharing. Give participants time to talk about their responses to questions 4-7, and ask them to save their index cards for later use.

After about five minutes, explain that while family members think they know one another very well, they often do not pay attention to one another on a daily basis. They sometimes fail to take the time to talk about subjects other than who needs to be where and when. Point out that deeper communication is necessary to maintaining and building relationships. Effective communication takes listening and understanding and requires that a family set aside time for conversation.

Move into the opening prayer by explaining that the group will begin by taking time for conversation with God, a vital member of our families who calls us into the family of God.

Opening Prayer

Read the Scripture Focus, page 34. Ask a member of the retreat team to prepare and lead a prayer asking God to be with the group and to bless the time that the group will spend together. If possible, close with a song such as "God's Circle of Love," from the cassette *Hi God 3*, Oregon Catholic Press, 800-548-8749.

At this point, those who are sixth-graders and younger leave the large group with the team leaders for their age groups.

7:30 pm

Presentation

Using the word *family* as an acronym, develop a presentation about what a family is and about what is involved in being a member of a family.

Introduce the talk by showing a picture of your family or another family and talking about the fact that families today take many different forms. Some are nuclear families, with mother, father, and a child or children. Others are single-parent families. Some families have been affected by divorce and the remarriage of the parents. They may be a blend of two families. Extended families are headed by grandparents, aunts or uncles, or other relatives who care for the children. Foster families care for children whose parents are unable to care for them. But no matter what the make-up of a family, its members need to take time to look at who they are, what they need, and how they can support one another.

Note: In developing the presentation, you will want to add personal stories to support the points being made. These personal stories could be told by the presenter or added by other retreat team members. Remember that these stories must be true. Do not make up a story just to make a point.

The following points may help you to develop the presentation that you will give in your own words.

For "F"
Fellowship: Family members can share with one another and spend quality-time together.

Friendship: Important and lasting friendships can develop between siblings. It would be good to support this point by adding a personal story about a family relationship that involves a friendship.

Note: Although the parent/child relationship can have elements of friendship, parents need to be parents to their children, not friends or buddies.

Forgiveness: Family members need to forgive one another. There are so many families in which members are at war with one another. In these families there is no growth, no fellowship, and, many times, no hope. When we ask the Lord for forgiveness in our personal lives and are reconciled to him, we grow in our fellowship with him. The same is true when we are willing to ask for and give forgiveness in our families.

Many Scripture passages could be used to support this point: Matthew 6:9-15 (the Lord's Prayer), Luke 15:11-32 (the parable of the prodigal son), Matthew 18:21-22 (Jesus' teaching on forgiveness). This is also a good point to insert a powerful witness talk on forgiveness in a family.

For "A"
Acceptance: Each of us is a unique person. Family members need to accept one another's uniqueness. Within our families, we should be free to be ourselves and be accepted as we are. Family members should also help one another to know and develop their unique gifts.

Awareness: Within our families, we need to be aware of one another, paying attention to one another's needs.

For "M"
Moods: We usually display our moods in our families. We feel free to "let our hair down" with our families. Unfortunately, that often leads to taking out our frustrations on family members. In addition, since our family members know us well, they usually know what "buttons" to push to set us off.

For "I"

Identity: Each of us has an identity in our family. At a family reunion, wedding or funeral, we usually explain who we are by saying who our grandparents, parents, or brothers and sisters are.

We also have an identity in the family of God. We are children of God and will forever be sons and daughters of God (Romans 8:15-17).

For "L"

Love: Love is a very misused and overused word. We say that we *love* pizza, we *love* this house, we *love* baseball or basketball or football. Actually love is a powerful emotion. We need to learn about the kind of love that Jesus teaches, the kind of love that we read about in 1 Corinthians 13:4-7.

Often family members take their love for one another for granted. This is a mistake. Each of us needs to know that we are loved. We can't be afraid to say "I love you" to those who mean the most to us. We also need to be aware that love involves hard work. It takes a lot of effort to love someone who has just done something we don't like. Family members need to be willing to put forth the effort.

For "Y"

You: Without *You*, there would be no *Family*. You are an important part of the family, and your family needs you to be an active member. The family of God also needs you. Each of us is a member of the family of God, with an active role to play in the family (Romans 15:5-7).

Summarize by pointing out that a family is made up of members working together. When family members are aware of one another and come to know the unique gifts of each member, they grow into true acceptance and fellowship. In the worst of moods or the best of moods, family members love one another and forgive one another. Among family members, there is an enduring commitment to and sense of responsibility for one another's well-being. The family is the support system that is central to the Church and society.

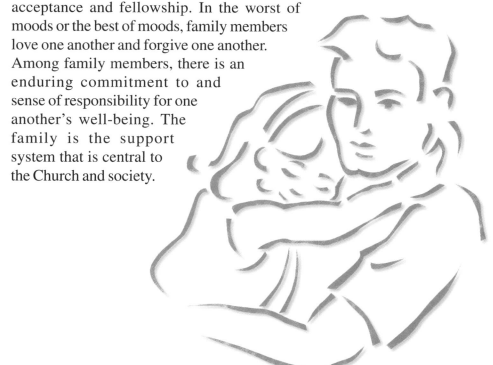

Who's in the House?

Small-Group Sharing

Ask participants to form groups of eight or fewer members. Provide directions for where each group will be meeting. Ask one member of each group to begin by offering a prayer asking the Lord to bless the group's conversation and time together.

Teen Small Groups

Option 1

"Eight Squares" is a good activity for seventh- and eighth-graders. Give each a half-sheet of paper, and have them fold it into eight squares.

Have teens number the squares 1-8 in any order they want. Tell them you will ask them a question for each square. They are to write their answers in the squares. Use these or similar questions.

1	3	5	7
2	4	6	8

1. List the members of your family in order of their ages, beginning with the oldest.
2. Which of your family's traditions is your favorite?
3. What TV family is your family most like? What character are you?
4. What idea from the presentation impressed you most?
5. Name one thing you like about your family.
6. Name one thing you would like to change about your family.
7. On a scale of 1-10, with 1 being the lowest and 10 being the highest, how would you rate the role that God plays in your family? Why?
8. Write a one-sentence definition that tells what family means to you.

When everyone has finished writing, invite teens to share their answers. You may wish to ask them to take turns sharing their answers to each question in turn. Or you may want to have each teen share all the answers on his or her sheet. Remember to have them introduce themselves before they share.

Option 2

You could use this activity with small groups of either younger or older adolescents. In their small groups, have teens introduce themselves, list the members of their family, describe their position in their families (oldest, youngest, and so on), and share their favorite family activity.

Then call on individual teens, asking them what ideas from the presentation they agree with, which they disagree with, and what idea impressed them most. Make sure that every member of the group has a chance to participate. Then review the acronym, asking teens what words they would add.

Close the small-group sharing with either of these activities.

Option 1

Ask participants to write responses to the following or similar questions. If you chose Option 2 for the community-building activity (page 36), participants can write on the back of their index cards and keep the cards for use during Family Prayer Time.

- What three words would you use to describe your family?
- If Jesus had dinner at your house tomorrow night, what do you think he would say to your family?
- If you were composing a prayer for your family, what would you pray for?

Option 2

Ask participants to write letters to Jesus, telling him about their families and their families' needs. Explain that these letters will be used during Family Prayer Time.

Adult Small Groups

Ask adults to form groups of eight or fewer members. If possible, assign a retreat team member to each group to lead the sharing.

If this is not possible, gather the adults as a large group to explain the process for the small-group sharing. Lead them in an opening prayer in the large group, and then have them form their small groups. Provide a copy of the questions for sharing for each group or parent. Encourage group members to take about five minutes to introduce themselves to one another before they begin.

Groups can use these or similar questions for sharing.

- How many members were there in your family of origin? How many members are in the family you parent?
- What is the greatest joy of being a parent?
- What is the most difficult struggle a parent faces?
- What surprised you most about being a parent?
- What ideas from the presentation do you agree with? What ideas do you disagree with? What ideas impressed you most?
- What ideas would you add to the presentation?
- What ideas would you like to share with other parents? Do you have hints about family communication, family time, gathering for meals, family prayer?

Close small-group sharing time with either of these activities.

Option 1

Ask parents to write their responses to the following questions. If you chose Option 2 for the community-building activity (page 36), participants can write on the back of the index cards and keep their cards for use during Family Prayer Time.

- What three words would you use to describe your family?
- If Jesus had dinner at your house tomorrow night, what do you think he would say to your family?
- If you were composing a prayer for your family, what would you pray for?

Option 2

Ask participants to write letters to Jesus, telling him about their families and their families' needs. Explain that these letters will be used during Family Prayer Time.

. . . .

Before the break, explain to adults the procedure for the family prayer that will follow the break. For prayer time, families will sit together as family units. There will be a short explanation and then time for families to share and pray together. First family members will share the responses they wrote for the first two questions.

- What three words would you use to describe your family?
- If Jesus had dinner at your house tomorrow night, what do you think he would say to your family?

Then families will be asked to come up with two action plans to help them grow as families. They may decide to:

- Institute family night once a week.
- Cook and share a special meal once a week.
- Select topics and schedule family discussion time.
- Work as a family to serve a need within their communities—school, parish, neighborhood, church.
- Plan family prayer time once a week.
- Include family affirmation time in one family activity every week.

Each family will be asked to write their plans down. Then families will have time to pray together. One suggestion is for family members to join hands and have each person say a thank-you to God for one gift he or she receives from the family. Prayer time could close with the Our Father and a family hug.

8:25 pm *Snack Break*

All the younger children rejoin their families.

Retreats for Teens

8:40 pm   Family Prayer Time

If possible, move to the church or chapel. Ask parents and kids to gather in family units, with enough space between families to provide privacy.

Share the following ideas in your own words.

God has a plan and a purpose for all our families. God invites us to put Jesus at the center of our family life so that God can reveal his plan to us through Jesus. We have to work at putting Jesus at the center of our families so that he can help us strengthen our families. We can accomplish this by sharing quality family time, using affirming speech with one another, serving the community together, taking time to show our love for one another, and by taking time to pray together. So we take time now to share and pray together as families.

Ask families to begin by sharing the responses they wrote to the first two questions.

- What three words would you use to describe your family?
- If Jesus had dinner at your house tomorrow night, what do you think he would say to your family?

Or they can begin by sharing the letters they wrote to Jesus about their families.

Then ask each family to create and write down two action plans to strengthen the family. When they have finished, families can share prayer time according to their own plans.

Options

If you have time, you could begin the prayer time with a short skit that depicts a family situation. This would have to be prepared ahead of time, possibly by retreat team members or by teens with an interest in drama.

Another option would be to begin by showing a short segment of a television show or movie that presents a view of family. Or you could play the song, "Two Sets of Jones'," from the CD *WWJD: What Would Jesus Do,* Forefront Communications Group.

9:00 pm   Conclusion and Departure

Thank all for coming. If possible, have a packet of resource materials available for every family.

You and I

Theme: Friendship

Scripture Focus: John 15:12-17

Target Group: High school freshmen and sophomores

Purpose: To help young people use the model Jesus gives us to explore the true meaning of friendship.

Objectives: To help young people to • discover the true meaning of friendship • recognize the importance of sharing, caring, listening, risking, and trusting in friendship • use the model of Jesus' friendship to evaluate friendships in their lives

Materials: Markers • pens or pencils, one for each participant and retreat team member • large sheets of paper or poster board • newsprint • tape • chalkboard or erasable marker board • 8 ½ x 11 sheets of paper • "Help Wanted" ads from the newspaper, cut apart so that everyone can have a section to look at • copies of "The Friend," Appendix page 77, of "Line-Ups," Appendix pages 78 and 79, and of "How Do I Build My Friendships?" Appendix page 80, one for each participant and retreat team member • Bibles (if possible, one for each person) • small slips of paper • an empty shoebox or basket

Optional Materials: Empty boxes to symbolize building blocks • props and costumes for skits • recordings of songs about friends and friendship ("You've Got a Friend in Me" from the CD of the original soundtrack from the movie *Toy Story,* Disney, or "Friends" by Michael W. Smith, from the CD *The Wonder Years*, Reunion) • a CD or tape player

Preparations: Arrange to hold this daylong retreat in a room with an informal atmosphere.

Print each of these statements at the top of a large sheet of paper or poster board. Make sure that the paper is thick enough so that the ink from markers will not soak through the paper.

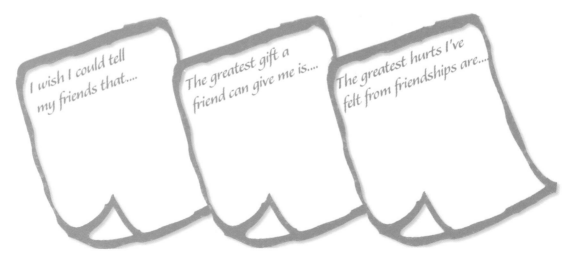

I wish I could tell my friends that....

The greatest gift a friend can give me is....

The greatest hurts I've felt from friendships are....

Post the three sheets of paper around the room so that teens can write on them. The sheets do not need to be next to one another.

9:00 am   Arrival and Welcome

Make sure retreat team members are on hand to meet and greet participants as they arrive.

9:15 am   Opening

Introduce the retreat director and the retreat team. Present the theme and objectives of the retreat and provide a brief overview of the day.

Community-Building Activity

Begin with the game "Who Are Your Friends?"

"Who Are Your Friends?"

Arrange chairs, carpet squares, or even sheets of colored paper in a circle. There should be one less place than there are participants.

Explain the game. One person, who will be "It," stands in the middle of the circle, with everyone else sitting in the circle. That person begins by saying, "Hi! My name is _____." Those sitting in the circle respond by saying, "Hi," and repeating the person's name. They also ask, "Who are your friends?"

The person in the middle of the circle responds, "My friends are people who _____," inserting a characteristic that describes at least five of the people in the circle. For example, those wearing jeans, those wearing red, and so on. All those who have been described must get up and find a new seat at least five seats from where they have been sitting. At the same time, "It" tries to find a seat, leaving a new "It" in the middle of the circle. Then the new "It" begins another round, following the same procedure.

Before you start the game, make sure everyone understands the directions. Continue the game for several rounds. Stop while teens are still enjoying the game.

If the person who is "It" has trouble getting a seat in the circle, suggest that he or she try to get everyone to change seats at the same time. This can be done by saying something like, "My friends are people who have noses," or "My friends are people who are on this retreat."

Opening Prayer

Ask a retreat team member to prepare and lead a prayer acknowledging the importance of friendship with God and with others, and asking God to bless the group's time together. Before the prayer, ask a volunteer to read aloud the Scripture Focus on page 44.

9:35 am   Message

Explain that to explore friendship, we first need to define *friend*. Give each participant a sheet of paper and a pen or pencil.

Distribute the sections of "Help Wanted" ads to the group. Read several ads aloud and then ask participants to write a "want ad" for a friend. When everyone has finished writing, ask for volunteers to share their ads with the group. To help young people feel comfortable, ask a retreat team member to begin the sharing.

After everyone who wants to has had a chance to read an ad, ask teens what they think the word *friend* means. Ask, How would you define *friend*? How would you define *friendship*? To give them a chance to reflect and gather their thoughts, have teens write answers to these questions.

Then ask teens to name their closest friends. Have teens list these friends' names or initials. Next to each name, teens are to write what qualities make this person a good friend.

9:50 am   *Introductory Small-Group Activity*

Ask participants to form groups of five to eight, with a member of the retreat team leading each group. Groups will need newsprint and markers. Give teens time to introduce themselves to everyone in their small group.

Ask for a volunteer, or appoint someone, to act as each group's secretary. Then have group members share their definitions of friend and friendship. The group's secretary is to record these definitions on newsprint so that everyone can refer to them. Then the group is to work together to write a definition of friend that everyone in the group agrees with, or that contains the elements that everyone feels are important. The secretary is to write the group's definition on a clean sheet of newsprint.

Each group should follow the same procedure to write a group definition of friendship. The secretary is to add this definition to the newsprint.

Option 1

Ask each group to consider the qualities that members have listed for their closest friends. Group members should take turns reading qualities from their lists, with the secretary recording them as they are given. If a quality is repeated, the secretary can add a check in front of the quality. After all the qualities are listed, the group should work together to pick the five qualities that they think are the most important. The secretary writes these five qualities—the group's top-five—under the definitions on the newsprint.

Option 2

Give each person a roll of pennies, a small container, and a copy of "The Friend," Appendix page 77. Ask teens to purchase the qualities they would want a friend to have, one penny for each quality. When everyone in the group has finished the exercise, ask each person to describe the ideal friend by listing the qualities he or she purchased and by telling everyone how much he or she spent. Then the groups should work to select the five qualities they think are most important in a friend. The secretary is to write these five qualities under the definitions on the newsprint.

Ask each group to choose one member to be the group's spokesperson.

10:30 am — Large-Group Sharing

Have each group's spokesperson read the group's definitions and top-five qualities, and post the group's newsprint where everyone can see it. When the large group has heard all small group reports, discuss similarities in the definitions and lists. If you have time, ask the large group to use components of the small groups' definitions and qualities lists to create large-group definitions and the large group's top-five qualities list.

Have a volunteer read Colossians 3:12-14. Ask teens to name the qualities they heard listed in this passage. As these qualities are named, write them on the chalkboard, marker board, or on newsprint for all to see. Ask, Which qualities are important in friends? How does this list compare with your top-five lists?

10:45 am — Message

Note: Before you begin this presentation, ask for volunteers to read the Scripture passages that will be used in the discussion. If possible, give volunteers time to prepare the readings.

Introduce teens to the story of the friendship between David and Jonathan (1 Samuel, chapters 17-20). This remarkable story can teach us much about the meaning of true friendship. David and Jonathan's friendship began on the day David defeated Goliath with a single stone (1 Samuel 17). Ask if anyone remembers and can retell the story of David and Goliath. Be prepared to have a team member fill in details that teens do not remember or to tell the story.

Then ask what teens know about Jonathan and Saul. Again, have a team member ready to provide information.

At this point, have volunteers read the Scripture passages that tell the story of the friendship of David and Jonathan. Introduce each reading with the short explanation.

- Jonathan makes a special covenant with David.
  Volunteer reads 1 Samuel 18:1-4.
- Jonathan makes a plea for David's life.
  Volunteer reads 1 Samuel 19:1-6.
- At this point, summarize chapter 20. Saul is very jealous of David and wants him dead. Their friendship leads David and Jonathan to take great risks for one another.
- Jonathan and David acknowledge the place of God in their friendship.
  Volunteer reads 1 Samuel 20:41-42.

Witness Talk

To make the Old Testament story of Jonathan and David more real for teens, ask for a volunteer to give a witness talk on the place of God in friendship, on the value of loyalty in friendship, or on the need for friends to make sacrifices for one another. For suggestions on developing a witness talk, see Appendix page 74.

Response

Ask the group what qualities of David and Jonathan made their friendship strong. First ask the group to list David's qualities from what they know of him. Using newsprint, a chalkboard, or a marker board, write the qualities down as they are given. Then ask the group to do the same for Jonathan. Make sure that everyone in the group can see the lists. Allow time for teens to compare these new lists with the top-five list they put together in their large-group sharing.

Wrap up by asking teens to discuss what role they think God plays in friendships.

Announcement

Before the group breaks for lunch, point out the three sheets of paper you posted around the room. See Preparations, page 44. Invite teens to write honest responses to the statements on the paper any time they have some free time. If they do not want anyone to know what they have written, they can write their responses on slips of paper. They should fold the slips in half and label the outside of each with a word that tells which statement the slip is for—wish, gift, or hurt. The slips can be dropped in the box or basket that you have provided. Explain that retreat team members will write the responses from the slips on the sheets of paper.

11:45 am Lunch

After lunch, make announcements to remind participants about completing the statements on the three sheets of paper, and to let them know when and where they will need to reconvene.

Recreation Break

1:00 pm Community-Building Activity

Refocus the group by bringing them all together to do a short community-building activity, such as "Line-ups," which provides a nonthreatening way for participants to get to know one another.

Point out an imaginary line, perhaps along one wall of the room. Explain that one end of the line will represent one extreme position on a topic and the other end the opposite extreme. The midpoint of the line will represent a moderate position.

Then announce one set of extremes. When you call "Go," participants are to take positions on the line that represent their positions on the topic. For examples of topics, see Appendix pages 78 and 79. Other examples can be added.

For other community-building activities, see *Getting Started: 100 Icebreakers for Youth Gatherings,* Appendix page 96.

1:20 pm

SHARING

CARING

LISTENING

RISKING

TRUSTING

Message—The Five Building Blocks of Friendship

Develop a twenty- to twenty-five-minute presentation on friendship. You may want to include some of these ideas about what friendship involves.

Sharing

There are many aspects of sharing involved in friendship, but sharing who we are and what we are about is the most basic to building relationships with others. As our sharing deepens, our friendship builds. The depth of the relationship we have with someone is dependent on the depth of our sharing.

Caring

What does it mean for us to care for another? Jesus gives us an example in the parable of the good Samaritan (Luke 10:25-37). Jesus begins the story by stating the greatest commandment—to love God and to love our neighbor. Then he uses the story of the selfless concern of the Samaritan for an injured stranger to tell us who our neighbors are and how we should care for them.

Listening

Have you ever tried to carry on a conversation with someone who never looked at you when you were talking? Or who never gave you a chance to share in the conversation? Or who never responded to anything you said? Conversations like these don't lead to genuine sharing and to deepening relationships. Because listening is very important in conversations, it is a skill that we need to learn and practice. It involves making eye contact with the person we are speaking to, focusing our attention on the person, and tuning out the distractions around us.

Risking

Jonathan took risks for his friend David. Although we probably will never be in as dramatic a situation as Jonathan and David were, we still face many risks in building friendships. It takes a risk to say "Hi" to everyone you pass in the hall at school, to sit at a lunch table with someone you don't know, to be the lab partner of someone new to your school, to tell someone your story. Jesus calls us to risks like these.

Trusting

Building trust is an important part of building friendships. Honesty is important to trust. Trust grows slowly as friends learn more about one another and as they respond positively to one another and to one another's needs.

Note: To personalize your presentation, add stories about friendships in your life or in the lives of someone you know. Invite retreat team members to add their own stories as well.

1:35 pm

Small-Group Response

Ask participants to rejoin their small sharing groups. Assign each group one of the five building blocks, and ask each group to create a five-minute skit to illustrate the importance of that building block.

Suggest that groups begin by discussing their building block. Have each person fill out the handout, "How Do I Build My Friendships?" Appendix page 80. Then group members can share and discuss their answers to the questions. Or the group leader could use the questions on the handout to lead the group's discussion.

After short discussions, groups can work on their skits. Groups could use their skits to show both the correct and incorrect ways of using their assigned building blocks in developing friendship.

2:30 pm *Skits/Showtime*
2:45 pm *Break*
3:00 pm *Message*

Jesus gives us the best examples of what friendships are all about. This is evident as we look at Jesus' relationships with his disciples, his followers, and Christians throughout the centuries.

Have participants read and discuss John 15:12-17. Include personal stories and/or have someone give a witness talk at the end of the presentation on how Jesus has been the model for friendship in his or her life.

"This is my commandment, that you love one another as I have loved you" (John 15:12).
• Name ways in which Jesus showed his love.

"No one has greater love than this, to lay down one's life for one's friends" (John 15:13).
• How would you define "self-sacrificing love"? Give examples, either from your own life or from experiences you have heard or read about.

"You are my friends if you do what I command you" (John 15:14).
• What do you think Jesus means when he says this?

"I do not call you servants any longer, because the servant does not know what the master is doing; but I have called you friends, because I have made known to you everything that I have heard from my Father" (John 15:15).
• Why is it important for friends to be open and honest with one another? Give examples to support your answer.
• Why do we sometimes wear different masks or assume different identities with different groups?

"You did not choose me but I chose you. And I appointed you to go and bear fruit, fruit that will last, so that the Father will give you whatever you ask him in my name" (John 15:16).
• Why is it an honor to have been chosen by Jesus?
• What do you think Jesus means when he tells his disciples to "go and bear fruit"? What do you think this has to do with us?

"I am giving you these commands so that you may love one another" (John 15:17).

- What kind of a friend am I to others? Give yourself a letter grade for each of your important friendships.

Summarize by pointing out that loving others in a self-sacrificing way—being willing to do what others want, being open and honest, and taking the first step to reach out—are all important parts of friendship. Jesus has done these things, and through him, we can do these things, too. In addition, Jesus will always be the greatest friend we could ever have.

3:30 pm

Reconciliation Service or Personal Prayer Time

Allow participants time for quiet individual prayer. If possible, arrange to use a church or chapel. Give each participant copy of "Pray.com," Appendix page 81. Ask them to follow this guide. Suggest that they make their friendships the focus of their prayer time.

If possible, provide an opportunity for teens to celebrate the sacrament of Penance. If that is not possible, celebrate forgiveness with a prayer service. See Appendix page 82.

Another option would be to have teens work together to create a prayer service that stresses ways to strengthen friendships, including with Jesus.

5:00 pm

Dinner

Announcements

Make announcements to let teens know who is responsible for clean-up and when they are to gather for the next activity.

5:45 pm

Affirmations or Liturgy

Ask each participant to write a note of affirmation to a friend. Give participants some suggestions to help them get started. For example, suggest that they write about the qualities of their friends that they most appreciate. Or they could write about times when their friends helped them get through difficult situations.

If possible, provide an opportunity for participants to celebrate a Liturgy together. Participants can take turns reading their affirmation notes after Communion.

If it is not possible to celebrate Mass, the affirmations can be read as part of the closing prayer.

6:30 pm

Sending Forth

Have participants sit in a large circle, and ask them to take turns sharing how they feel about the retreat. To help teens get started, begin the sharing yourself, or ask another retreat team member to begin.

Closing Prayer

Ask teens to remain in their circle, and explain that they are going to create their own litany of friends. Teens may be familiar with the litany of saints that is part of the Easter Vigil. For those who are not familiar with this prayer form, explain that a litany is a series of prayers and responses. For example:

All: We pray for the people who are important in our lives.

Each person mentions the name or initials of a friend.

For _____,

Response: Hear our prayer, Jesus, our friend.

Encourage teens to create their own form for the litany. After the litany, participants can share their affirmation notes.

7:00 pm   Departure

The Search

Theme: Looking at who we are and who Jesus is in our lives.

Scripture Focus: 2 Corinthians 13:5 or Matthew 13:3-9 and 13:18-23

Target Group: High school juniors and seniors

Purpose: To give teens an opportunity to think about who they are and what they believe in.

Objectives: To help teens to • understand who they are and what they believe in • enter into a deeper personal relationship with Jesus • develop a plan for continued faith growth

Materials: Markers and pens or pencils, one for each participant and retreat team member • Bibles, one for each participant • lunch bags, one for each participant and retreat team member • small slips of paper, several for each participant and retreat team member • notebooks or sheets of writing paper • a whistle or bell or some other device to call time • a tape or CD player • a recording of soft instrumental music • copies of "Pray.com," Appendix page 81, one for each participant and retreat team member • TV and VCR • a copy of the video, *Indiana Jones and the Last Crusade* • copies of an evaluation form for each participant and retreat team member, Appendix page 85

Optional Materials: Props and costumes for skits

Preparations: Work through "The Five Ws and One H for Planning Retreats," and prepare the checklist on Appendix page 71. Provide a copy of the completed checklist for each member of the retreat team.

If the retreat team wants participants to receive letters from their parents during this retreat, contact parents ahead of time. For suggestions on how to do this, see "Care Letters," page 12, and Appendix page 87.

Friday

Note: It's best to have the retreat team arrive before the participants. This allows time for setup, for taking care of last-minute details, and for prayer. If all team members cannot be present for prayer before the retreat begins, consider gathering for prayer while the director of the retreat facility acquaints participants with the facility and its guidelines.

7:00 pm

Arrival and Welcome

Make sure members of the retreat team are available to meet and greet teens and to show them to the sleeping areas. Allow time for participants to unpack their gear and get settled.

7:30 pm

Opening

Invite the director or a representative of the retreat facility to speak with the participants about the facility and its rules or guidelines.

Then introduce the retreat director and the retreat team. Present the theme and the objectives of the retreat and provide a brief overview of the weekend. It's helpful to post a schedule that participants can refer to.

If the retreat team has chosen a song to support the theme of the retreat, introduce and, if necessary, teach it to participants. If the team has chosen symbols or slogans for the weekend, display these in some appropriate form— pictures, photos, banners, actual objects.

Opening Prayer

Open the retreat with prayer. Ask a member of the retreat team to prepare a prayer placing the retreat participants in God's hands and asking for God's blessing on the group's time together. Have another retreat team member or a teen volunteer begin the prayer by reading the passage the retreat team chose for the Scripture Focus on page 53.

Community-Building Activity

Choose this activity based on how well participants know one another. For groups whose members don't know one another well, choose an activity that will help teens to get to know one another's names. Select from among the "Getting Acquainted" activities in *Getting Started: 100 Icebreakers for Youth Gatherings.* See Appendix page 96.

For groups whose members know one another, choose an activity that will help them to get to know one another better. You could use "Line-ups" or a variation of this activity. See page 48 and Appendix pages 78 and 79 in this book. Or select an activity from among the "Thought Provokers" activities in *Getting Started: 100 Icebreakers for Youth Gatherings.*

Introductory Small-Group Activity

Before the retreat, team members can assign participants to small groups and decide where each group will meet. Listed here are some ways to let participants know about their small-group assignments. To use any of these suggestions, write teens' names on small envelopes. Put into each envelope the item that will designate that person's group. Hand out the envelopes and ask participants and group leaders to find the others whose items match theirs.

- Print participants' names on nametags, using a different colored or shaped nametag for each group. Or each nametag can have a small number, colored dot, or other identifying mark on it. Ask participants to look for others with the same kind of nametag.
- Make puzzles, one for each small group. Use the pictures from an old calendar. Glue a picture onto poster board. Draw puzzle-piece shapes on the poster board, one piece for each member in the group, including the leader(s), and cut out the pieces. Group members need to look for all the pieces that complete the picture.
- Cut the panels of a comic strip apart, with one panel for each group member. Participants need to find the other panels that complete the strip.
- Give group members slips of paper with the names of objects of the same color. The group leader's slip should name the color. Group members are to look for others whose objects are the same color as theirs. For example, members of the orange group might receive slips naming objects such as oranges, construction cones, pumpkins, basketballs, carrots, tangerines, marshmallow circus peanuts.

Have participants join their small groups, with team members serving as group leaders. Ask group leaders to follow the guidelines for small-group sharing, pages 20 and 21. Group leaders should be prepared to offer the opening prayer for this first meeting, but then ask for volunteers to take turns doing the prayers.

Help group members get to know one another by sharing information about themselves. For example, the group leader could call out a question, and then all members of the group could take turns answering the question. Begin with simple nonthreatening questions: What is your name? Where do you go to school? What is your favorite kind of music? Time of day? Food? If you could live anywhere in the world, where would you live?

If there is time, group leaders can move from asking basic getting-to-know-you-questions to questions such as: Why did you decide to do this retreat? What would you like to gain from this retreat? If you were asked to rate your faith on a scale of 1-10, with 10 being the strongest, what number would you use? Why?

8:45 pm Large-Group Activity /Optional

Use this activity if participants need to get to know one another better. Ask small groups to sit together in the large-group area. Members of each small group should pick one thing they have learned about one another to share with the large group—for example, favorite foods. Each member of the small group introduces the person to his or her right to the large group, saying that person's name and favorite food.

9:00 pm Snack Break

9:30 pm Message—The Search for Who We Are

Note: During the presentation, you will be using a lunch bag to represent you, and you will need to prepare the bag ahead of time. On the outside of the bag, write words or draw pictures that represent things you know about yourself that are easy to share with others—gifts, talents, interests, concerns, hang-ups, beliefs, things that are important to you. On the bottom of the bag, write words or draw pictures that show some decisions or actions you are not proud of—smoking, lying, abusing drugs or alcohol.

Put inside the bag things that are more difficult to share. On small slips of paper, write words that represent some of these things—dreams, fears, secrets, hurts, joys, and so on.

In developing your presentation, use your own words to make these points.

We need to look at who we are. We are very busy people. We fill our time with many activities. Often we don't take time to stop and think about who we are, what we truly believe in, and what our questions, concerns, and fears are.

We are usually quick to make judgments about people based on our first impressions of them. Many times we make assumptions about who people are and what they are all about without even speaking to them. If possible, add a personal story as an example of a time when you made a judgment about someone that turned out not to be true, or of a time when someone else did this to you.

What we see on the outside often does not reveal who the person truly is. A person's appearance is a shell. It is only when we allow ourselves to listen to one another that we begin to know who someone truly is.

Many times we don't know our own story. Our stories make us the persons we are. But sometimes we are not sure who we are. To make matters even more complicated, we sometimes wear masks, pretending to be one person for one group and another person for another group. Sometimes the person on the outside—the person we show others—is the person we feel it is safe to be. But the person on the inside is the real person. Use the lunch bag you prepared to demonstrate. Point out your gifts and talents and some things you are not proud of. Reach into the bag and pull out and read a couple of the slips that represent things that are more difficult for you to share.

Knowing that God created us can help us feel safe to be ourselves. Read aloud Psalm 139:13-15. Give teens time to consider what this Scripture passage means for them. Write these or similar questions on the chalkboard or on a large sheet of newsprint so that everyone can see them. Ask teens to journal answers to these questions. Be sure teens know that no one will see their answers. This exercise is for their own benefit.

- Who am I ?
- What are my gifts and talents?
- What do I like? What do I dislike?
- What do I fear?
- When was I the happiest I have ever been? Why?
- What are my favorite things?
- What are the best things about my personality?
- What is something I want or need to change about myself?
- Whom do I most admire? Why?
- How do my parents see me? How do my friends see me? How do I see myself?
- What blessings has God given me?

10:00 pm   *Individual Activity*

Give each person a lunch bag. Have markers, pens, and pencils available. Ask participants to make bags representing themselves. Explain that on the outside of the bag, they are to write words or draw pictures that represent the things about themselves that they find easy to share with others—gifts, talents, interests, concerns, hang-ups, beliefs, things that are important to them. Provide small slips of paper. Give participants the option to write or draw on the slips things they find more difficult to share with others. These slips go inside their bags. Remind teens to put their names on their bags.

Give participants a time limit so they will get to work right away. If possible, have soft instrumental music playing in the background.

10:20 pm   *Small-Group Sharing*

Have participants rejoin their small groups, and remind them to open and close with brief prayers. Encourage members of the small groups to get to know one another better by sharing what they have written on their bags. If they feel comfortable doing so, they can also share the more sensitive information they have placed inside the bags.

Night Prayer

Ask participants to gather as a large group. Explain that their bags will now serve as Palanca Bags. Use the information on page 13 for your explanation. Select a place that will be accessible to all participants, and have participants leave their bags there to hold the affirmation notes that participants will be writing during the course of the weekend.

Make any necessary announcements for bedtime and morning procedures. End with the Living Rosary, page 25, or the following prayer.

The Gift

Materials: A Bible • a candle to represent the light of Christ • a small box, preferably wooden with a hinged cover • a mirror that fits inside the box • a tape or CD player • a recording of an appropriate song, such "Here I Am" by Tom Booth, from the CD *Find Us Ready*, Oregon Catholic Press, 800-548-8749, or "Step by Step" by Rich Mullins, from the CD *The World as Best I Remember It*, Reunion.

Open by sharing a sign of peace or by playing a song.

Leader: God has given each of us a treasure, a gift that is unique to each of us. Inside this box is the gift. Take turns opening the box and reflecting on the gift you find there. Then close the box and pass it to the next person.

As the box is being passed, play some soft instrumental music. After everyone has had a chance to open the box, the leader continues.

Leader: Tonight we are taking time out to search for who we are. There's an old proverb that says, "What you are is God's gift to you. What you become is your gift to God." Please listen to God's description of how well he knows each of us.

The leader reads the following paraphrased version of Psalm 139, inserting names of retreat participants in the blanks.

Psalm 139

_____, I have examined you and I know you.

_____, I know when you sit and when you stand.

_____, I know all that you do.

_____, I understand your thoughts.

_____, I am acquainted with all your ways.

_____, before a word is on your tongue, I know what you will say.

_____, where can you hide from my spirit?

_____, where can you hide from my presence?

_____, I am with you always and everywhere.

_____, if you were to journey to the sunrise or sail beyond the sea, my hand will guide you.

_____, I formed the depths of your being.

_____, I knit you together in your mother's womb.

_____, you are wonderfully made.

Leader: Reflect on what help you need from God to know who you are. Think of a word or two to say as a petition that asks God for the gift you need.

Pause.

Leader: As the candle that signifies Christ's light is passed to you, please share your petition. Then pass the candle on.

All share petitions and join together to respond to each petition.

Response: We place our prayers in God's hands.

11:25 pm
12:00 am

Preparations for Bedtime
Lights Out

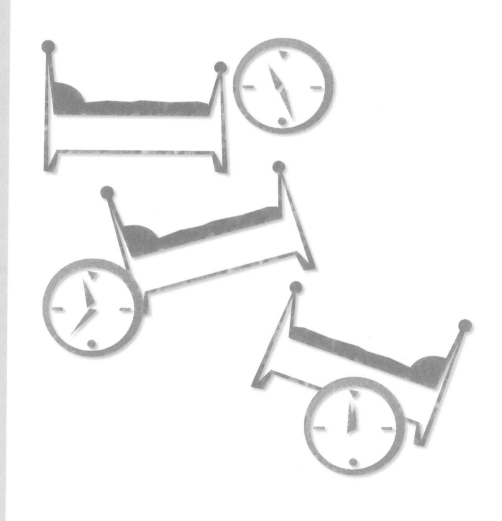

Saturday

8:00 am	**Wake-up Call**
8:30 am	**Retreat Team Meeting and Prayer**

The retreat team can begin with a prayer for the success of the morning's work. They can also use a few minutes to discuss how the retreat is going, deal with any problems, and go over the morning's schedule.

9:00 am	**Breakfast**
10:00 am	**Large-Group Gathering**
	Morning Prayer

Use a song that will get everyone moving, such as "Big House" by Audio Adrenaline, from the CD *Don't Censor Me*, Forefront Communications Group. Teach the actions that go with the words of the song's refrain before you begin the prayer.

Use these actions for the refrain, "Come and go with me to my Father's house."

> *Come*—hands wave toward self, inviting others to come
> *and go with me*—point index figure at self
> *to*—hold up two fingers on each hand
> *my*—point index finger at self
> *Father's*—point both index fingers toward the sky
> *house*—move hands away from sides with palms facing in and put palms together above the head

Use these actions for this line, "It's a big, big house, with lots and lots of room, a big, big table with lots and lots of food."

> *It's a big, big*—with hands in front of chest, move palms away from each other to signify big
> *house*—see "house," above
> *with lots and lots of room*—raise hands above head and wave them as body sways
> *a big, big*—see "It's a big, big," above
> *table*—hold hands with palms toward the floor and cross hands in front of chest to signify the surface of a table
> *with lots and lots of food*—use hands to signify putting food in the mouth

Use these actions for this line, "A big, big yard where we can play football."

A big, big—see "a big, big," page 60
yard—clasp hands and then pull them apart as far as possible to signify yard
where we can play football—pretend to throw a football pass

Repeat actions for these lines, "A big, big house. It's my Father's house." For the verses, clap to the beat.

When everyone has had a chance to practice these motions, play the song and have them put the actions to the song's words.

Read or have a volunteer read John 14:1-3.

Ask a retreat team member to offer a spontaneous prayer for the success of the day.

10:30 am   Message—The Search for God

Introduce this presentation by showing the three tests of faith from the film *Indiana Jones and the Last Crusade*. Scan the video ahead of time so you can cue it to begin after Indiana Jones' father has been shot. At that point, Indiana Jones must save his father by passing the tests of faith and reaching the Holy Grail.

Or produce your own video introduction by doing person-on-the-street interviews, asking five or six people what they believe in, what gives their lives meaning.

Continue the presentation on the search for God by having a retreat team member do a witness talk on his or her personal search for God. Provide a copy of "Developing a Witness Talk," Appendix page 74, to help this team member prepare. Introduce the witness talk by reading aloud John 3:16-18.

11:00 am   Small-Group Discussion

Ask teens to return to their small groups, and remind them to begin and end with prayer.

If you showed a portion of the Indiana Jones film, ask teens to discuss these or similar questions.

- What was the first test of faith? What does it mean to be humble? How can we develop the virtue of humility?
- What was the second test? What are the ways we can walk in the footsteps of God?
- What was the third test? A leap of faith involves complete trust. Is it easy or difficult for you to put your trust in God? Why? Have you ever been asked to make a leap of faith?
- What do you think keeps us from trusting in God? From experiencing his love for us?

Include questions about the witness talk.
- What do you think John is telling us in this passage?
- What one thing from the witness talk impressed you most? Why?

11:45 am ## Personal Prayer Time

Ask participants to move to a quiet place that provides enough room so that they can all spread out for privacy and comfort. A church or chapel would be ideal.

Give participants copies of "Pray.com," Appendix page 81, and ask them to follow these suggestions for spending time with God.

12:15 pm ## Small-Group Discussion

Ask participants to join their small groups to discuss their reactions to their experiment with personal prayer.

12:30 pm ## Lunch

1:15 pm ## Retreat Team Meeting and Prayer

The retreat team can spend a few minutes discussing how the retreat is going, dealing with any problems, and going over the afternoon's schedule. They can end with a prayer for the success of the afternoon's work.

1:30 pm ## Large-Group Gathering
Community-Building Activity

Choose an activity that will serve to reconnect everyone and help them to focus on the retreat's theme. Here's a suggestion.

Michelangelo Sculptures

1. Have teens pair up, preferably with someone they do not know well. Ask partners to introduce themselves to each other and find out whose birthday comes first in the year.
2. The partner whose birthday is first is the great Michelangelo, painter and sculptor. The other partner is a lump of clay. Lumps of clay are not able to speak.
3. Michelangelo's job is to form his lump of clay into a sculpture that expresses an emotion. Lumps of clay are to cooperate, moving according to the directions of Michelangelo. The Michelangelos have ten seconds to sculpt their lumps of clay. When teens hear the ten-second whistle, clay forms are to freeze in position and Michelangelos are to sit down so that everyone can admire the sculptures.
4. In the first round, Michelangelos form lumps of clay into sculptures depicting extreme "JOY." Time ten seconds, do a five-second countdown, and then blow the whistle. Clay forms freeze and Michelangelos sit down. Invite teens to make comments about the sculptures. They might pretend that they are art critics, but remind them that all comments are to be kind and respectful.
5. For the next round, lumps of clay and Michelangelos switch roles. Michelangelo's job is to mold his clay into a sculpture depicting unbelievable, without-a-doubt "FEAR." Time ten seconds, do a five-second countdown, and then blow the whistle. Clay forms freeze and Michelangelos sit down. Invite teens to make comments about the sculptures.

6. Ask each pair to join with another pair to form groups of four. Members of these new groups are to introduce themselves to one another and find out which two people's birthdays are first in the year. These two will be Michelangelos. Explain that there will now be two lumps of clay and two Michelangelos. The Michaelangelos are to work together to form the lumps of clay into a sculpture depicting "TRUST." Time fifteen seconds, do a five-second countdown, and blow the whistle. Clay forms freeze and Michelangelos sit down. Allow art-critic comments.

7. The Michelangelos and the lumps of clay switch roles. Michelangelos are to mold their clay into a sculpture depicting "COMPANIONSHIP." Time fifteen seconds, do a five-second count-down, and blow the whistle. Clay forms freeze, and Michelangelos sit down and make comments about the sculptures.

8. Ask each group of four to join another group to form groups of eight. Members of the newly formed groups introduce themselves to one another. Then explain that everyone will now be both Michelangelos and lumps of clay at the same time. That means they will have to work together to form a sculpture using all eight people. Each group needs to select one person to act as the group spokesperson to explain their sculpture. Before the sculpting begins, have all the spokespersons raise their hands so that you can be sure that all the groups have one.

9. Announce that the groups are to form sculptures depicting "THE SEARCH." Time twenty-five seconds, announce fifteen seconds, do a five-second countdown, and blow the whistle. All freeze.

10. Go group by group, asking the spokesperson to explain the group's sculpture. When a group has explained its sculpture, its members can sit and watch as the other groups' sculptures are explained.

Close by making the following statement or putting this statement into the form of a prayer.

As we SEARCH this weekend, we hope to be able to ease some of our FEAR—fear about our relationship with God, about being on retreat, about being honest and open, and about placing our fear in God's hands. We also need to learn to TRUST God and others. Companions are important in our search. We all need to have COMPANIONSHIP in our lives—especially in our SEARCH for faith. Let's continue to support one another and to place ourselves in God's hands. Then we will be able to allow more of God's JOY into our lives.

Message—The Search for a Relationship with Jesus

This presentation will focus on how having a relationship with Jesus can affect a person and that person's other relationships. Developing this theme will involve personal stories and could certainly include witness talks. Try to include these related Scripture passages in your presentation: Matthew 13:3-9, Matthew 16:13, and John 3:16-18.

You will want the presentation to include the following points:

• A description of who Jesus is for the speaker
• An explanation of head knowledge and heart knowledge
• A statement of why the speaker(s) wants to have a relationship with Jesus
• A statement of how God desires to be in relationship with us

2:00 pm

Small-Group Discussion

Have participants join their small groups, and remind the groups to begin and end with prayer. Use the information given in the presentation to develop questions for small-group leaders to use. Here are some suggestions.

- What five words would you use to describe Jesus? Why?
- How would you describe who Jesus is for you?
- What's the difference between head knowledge and heart knowledge?
- Does your relationship with Jesus involve more head knowledge or heart knowledge? Why?
- What does John 3:16-18 tell us about our relationship with Jesus?
- What does John 3:16-18 tell us about why God wants to be in relationship with us?
- Matthew 13:3-9 is called the parable of the sower. What does this parable mean to you?
- What kind of soil do you think you are at this time? Why?
- How would you answer the question that Jesus asks in Matthew 16:13?
- On a scale of 1 (distant) to 10 (very close), what number best describes your relationship with Jesus at present?
- In what ways are you seeking to have a relationship with Jesus?

2:45 pm

Large-Group Organized Game

Following is just one suggestion. Many options are available.

Clue Hunt

Materials: A list of at least ten to twelve words for the teams to draw • sheets of writing paper and pens or pencils

1. Explain the rules. Each group will be a team, and teams will compete with one another. Team members are to draw clues that will help their group guess a word. Clues should be pictures. No writing letters, words, or numbers, and no talking will be allowed. The group who guesses all the clues first, and correctly, is the winner.

2. Have participants join their small groups. Allow each small group to choose its own area to work in within the large-group area. The members in each small group should count off, with each person's number indicating the order in which group members will participate. Each group should write the numbers from 1 to 10 or 12, depending on how many you choose for the game, down the left side of a sheet of paper.

3. Explain that the person who is Number 1 from each group will go the clue-giver and get a clue. That person will go back to the group and draw the clue. The rest of the small group will try to guess the word. Warn the groups to work quietly so the other groups will not overhear what they are saying. When the group guesses the first word, Number 1 person writes the word next to the Number 1 on the group's sheet of paper. The word is only to be written on the paper when the group has guessed it. Then Number 2 person goes to the clue-giver to get the second clue, taking the sheet of paper along so that the clue-giver will know the last word the group received. Number 2 person brings a second clue back to the group, and the process is repeated. Groups

follow the same procedure as quickly as possible until all the clues have been given out and the groups have finished guessing the clues. The groups call out "Done" when they have guessed their last clues. One of the retreat team members can keep track of who finishes first, second, and third. When all the groups are finished, the clue-giver can quickly check the answers of the group who finished first to see if their answers are correct. If not, the clue-giver checks the answers of the group who finished second. If they have more correct answers, they will have won.

4. To make the game more difficult, the clue-giver will not be stationary. The clue-giver will find different spots to hide in so that group members will need to find the clue-giver before they can receive their clues. Set boundaries for the clue-giver and let everyone know what these are. For example, the clue-giver, who is a member of the retreat team, should not hide in bathrooms or sleeping areas and should not make hiding places so difficult to find that the game will be drawn out.

5. Award a prize to the winning group, maybe a bag of candy that the group members can share.

Announcements

After the game, remind participants to keep writing their palancas. Make any other necessary announcements. For example, let participants know how long their break will be and where they will need to be after the break is over.

Break

Retreat Team Meeting and Prayer

The retreat team can spend a few minutes discussing how the retreat is going, dealing with any problems, and going over the schedule for the rest of the day. They can end with a prayer for the success of the day's work.

5:00 pm ## Small-Group Activity—Skit Preparation

Ask participants to rejoin their small groups to prepare skits based on one of the presentations or the theme of the retreat. Encourage teens to have fun with this project. For example, groups could do take-offs on game shows or sitcoms.

Make sure that group leaders are aware of the guidelines for skits on page 17, and that the leaders share these guidelines with their groups. Urge leaders to participate in creating and putting on the skits.

6:00 pm ## Dinner

Announcements

6:45 pm

Message—The Search for Healing and Forgiveness

Begin this presentation by reading aloud Matthew 18:21-35. Developing this theme will involve personal stories and could certainly include witness talks. Use the following points in developing your presentation:

- What I relate to most in this Scripture passage
- What forgiveness means to me
- What walls I put up between God and myself and between myself and others
- What I need forgiveness for
- What hurts I need healing for

Try to include in your presentation that we sometimes fail to ask for God's forgiveness because we think that we have done something that God cannot forgive. The truth is that there is nothing that God cannot forgive (1 John 1:9). When we try to justify, excuse, or explain our sinful choices and decisions away, our actions prevent us from experiencing God's love (1 John 1:8).

7:00 pm

Small-Group Discussion

Ask teens to discuss what sin, forgiveness, and reconciliation mean to them. After about five minutes, group leaders should explain that the next activity will be a reconciliation service. They should explain what will be involved, especially if there will be the opportunity for participants to celebrate the sacrament of Penance with individual confession and absolution. Since teens will have varying levels of comfort and familiarity with the sacrament of Penance, group leaders will need to be sure to take time to answer any questions teens may have. The book *A Time and Place for Healing: The Sacrament of Penance for Teens* may be helpful. See Appendix page 96.

7:30 pm

Reconciliation and Healing Service

On Appendix page 82, you will find a reconciliation service to use or adapt. During this service, schedule time give for participants to receive their letters from their parents.

9:00 pm

Break

Teens can use this short break to go to the bathroom and to finish up planning for the skits.

9:30 pm

Skits/Showtime

10:00 pm

Snack Break and Free Time

11:30 pm

Preparations for Bedtime

12:00 am

Lights Out

Sunday

8:00 am   ## Wake-up Call

8:30 am   ## Retreat Team Meeting and Prayer

The retreat team may need to spend some time working out details for activities of the day, particularly the Liturgy. For suggestions for planning the Liturgy, see page 68. Team members can end with a prayer for the success of the retreat.

9:00 am   ## Breakfast

Announcements

Remind participants that they will need to pack up their personal belongings before they gather for prayer.

10:00 am   ## Morning Prayer

Use the morning prayer suggested on page 24.

10:15 am   ## Large-Group Gathering

Call the group together and explain the next small-group activity, "Affirmation Circles," page 14. The retreat team members will know participants well enough now to be able to select the option that will best suit the group.

Small-Group Activity—Affirmation Circles

Note: Small groups will probably finish this activity at different times. If each small group is helping to plan the Liturgy, when a group finishes with its affirmations, it can begin to work on Liturgy planning. Or each group could be assigned an area for clean-up

11:00 am   ## Message—Carry Out the Search

Have participants work as a large group to summarize the retreat. Do this by asking participants to say what they have learned during the retreat. As points are given, write them on a chalkboard or on newsprint, large enough so that everyone can read them.

Individual Activity

Ask participants to write letters to themselves outlining plans for continuing the growth in faith that began in this retreat. Ask teens to be specific about what they intend to do. For example, if they feel they need to strengthen their connection with their faith community—their parish—they might pick one committee or activity they want to become involved in.

When everyone has finished writing, pass out envelopes and ask each participant to address an envelope to himself or herself. Their letters are to

be folded into the self-addressed envelopes and then sealed. Collect the letters and explain that you will mail the letters in about two months so that everyone can be reminded of their plans.

Have participants fill out and turn in evaluation forms. For a sample of an evaluation form, see Appendix page 85.

12:00 pm ## Lunch

After lunch, have participants do any necessary clean-up. If each small group is helping to plan the Liturgy, this would be a good time for them to finish their work.

1:00 pm ## Liturgy or Prayer Service

To involve each small group in planning the Liturgy, assign each group one of the following areas to be in charge of.

Environment: Arrange and decorate the physical space where the Liturgy will take place.

Consult with the priest and then prepare the altar with cloths, candles, and other necessary elements. Discuss with the priest how the gifts should be presented and make plans to carry this out.

Music: Choose and help lead the songs. Choose simple and familiar songs for the opening, psalm response (said or sung), eucharistic acclamations, presentation of the gifts, Communion, and the closing. Make sure songbooks are available, or ask the parish liturgist or musician to help you put together song sheets.

Readings: Determine how the readings will be proclaimed. They could be acted out, done as choral readings, or read in parts. Decide who the readers will be. If the Mass will be on a Sunday, you will need to do the readings of the day from the lectionary. If the Mass will be on another day, check with the priest for help on selecting readings.

Creed: Prepare a special Creed for the Liturgy by rewriting the Creed in your own words.*

Prayer Intercessions: Write and read the intercessions for the Liturgy.*

Communion Reflection: Write and read prayers of thanksgiving.*

* Check these with the priest.

Sending Forth

This can be done during the closing Liturgy or concluding prayer service. If the retreat includes Liturgy, the sending forth can be done following Communion. Have everyone take someone else's palanca bag. They are to hold onto these and not look in them.

The retreat director can ask participants to think about what this retreat has meant to them, pausing to allow a few moments for reflection. The retreat director can begin by sharing what the retreat has meant for him or her. After sharing, the retreat director calls up the person whose palanca bag he or she holds, gives that person a sign of affection—a hug or warm, firm handshake—and his or her palanca bag. That person repeats the process. This continues until everyone has his or her own bag. Ask participants not to look in their palanca bags until everyone has his or her own bag. If time permits, participants can read their affirmations. If time is short, participants can take their bags with them.

Note: If someone refuses to share or has a very hard time sharing, move on. Call on someone else who hasn't shared yet.

2:00 pm   ## Departure

Reviewing the Five Ws and the One H

WHO?

Who is the target group? _____

Who will be needed to help? _____

_____

WHY?

Why would this group benefit from a retreat? _____

_____

WHAT?

What theme is appropriate for this retreat? _____

What is the purpose of this retreat? _____

What objectives do we want to achieve? _____

_____

What format is best for this group and for accomplishing the retreat's purpose and objectives?

_____

WHEN?

When should the retreat be held? _____

_____

WHERE?

Where should the retreat be held? _____

_____

HOW?

How will the purpose and objectives of the retreat be accomplished?

Focus Area #1—Community Building

Icebreakers (or fire-starters) _____

_____

Affirmations _____

_____

Free Time and Break Schedule _____

_____

Focus Area #2—Message

Presentations and Witness Talks _____

_____

Other Activities _____

_____

Sending Forth _____

_____

Focus Area #3—Response

Large-Group Sharing _____

_____

Small-Group Sharing _____

_____

Other Activities _____

_____

Focus Area #4—Prayer and Worship

Opening Prayer _____

_____

Closing Prayer _____

_____

Liturgical Prayer _____

_____

Focus Area #5—Follow-up

Evaluations _____

_____

Other Plans _____

_____

Developing a Witness Talk

A witness talk is your personal account of how God has worked in your life. A witness talk is a way for you to give thanks for, give witness to, and let others know how God has worked in your life. Have confidence that God has worked in you. Let him use you so he can work in the lives of others.

To prepare a witness talk, answer the following questions, writing down everything that comes to you.

- What are some ways I have experienced God in my life?
- In what areas have I seen a change in my life because of my faith in and relationship with God?
- When I asked for help, how did God respond?
- What have I learned that others can relate to? What part did God play in what I have learned?
- Read the Scripture Focus of the retreat. What is this passage saying? What picture of God do I get from this passage? With what person or event do I identify most? In what ways do I relate to the Scripture Focus?

Then organize your thoughts using the steps given below.

Step One: A Picture of Your Life Before Your Conversion

- Select a situation in your life that relates to the Scripture Focus or the message of the retreat.
- State what you are sharing about and how it relates to the Scripture Focus or the message of the retreat.
- Describe the situation. (Note: Providing too many details can be distracting.)
- Own up to the mistakes you made in the situation.
- Try to establish an example that you can come back to.
- State how God worked in this situation.

Step Two: Conversion Point

- What circumstances caused you to turn to God?
- What did other people say or do that caused you to turn to God?
- Why did you decide to trust in God?
- What did you say?
- What did you do?
- How did God respond?

Step Three: A Picture of Your Life Now*

- Give examples that show in concrete ways how your life has changed.
- To emphasize how your life has changed, refer to the example you used in the first part of your witness talk.

* The truth is that once God has worked in your life, you are not the same. Your life is different—better, more complete, happier, more peaceful. But you are not perfect, nor is your life perfect. You

still have struggles and problems. You do not want to suggest in your witness talk that once you experienced the presence of God in your life, everything was perfect. You probably want to use phrases such as, "That was the first step for me…." "That day was a beginning for me…." "I was not the same after that day. I began to…."

Things to Keep in Mind

- Maintain good eye contact with your audience.
- Understand the difference between a witness talk and a presentation. A witness talk shares personal experience; a presentation provides information.
- Understand that our words do not have the power to change people. Change comes from the action of the Holy Spirit.
- Review your witness talk to make sure that it does not sound harsh or condemning.
- Tell the truth; don't manipulate facts.
- Be discreet about the personal information you reveal about yourself.
- Be open to feedback, constructive criticism; guard against oversensitivity and self-condemnation.
- Make notes about what you want to say. Use the notes to keep your witness talk on track.
- Record your witness talk and listen to it before you give it to the retreat group.
- Practice your witness talk in front of a mirror.

Stirrings of the Spirit

Guidelines for Praying with Scripture

Let no one despise your youth, but set the believers an example in speech and conduct, in love, in faith, in purity. Until I arrive, give attention to the public reading of scripture, to exhorting, to teaching.

1 Timothy 4:12–13

1. Before you begin, try, as much as possible, to let go of the distractions of the day and block out the noises around you. As your mind and spirit settle down and become more peaceful, recall that this time will be spent with God. Place yourself in God's presence. Begin in prayer, asking for the grace to open your heart to hear what God wants to say to you. Pray that the Holy Spirit will help you to respond willingly.

2. Read the Scripture passage. Be aware of the people, the setting, the atmosphere.

3. Reread the passage slowly and put yourself into the scene. Become a part of the passage.

4. Reflect on the passage you've just read.
   What does this passage mean?

   How does this passage help you to know God? What picture of God do you get from this passage?

   With what person or event do you identify most in this passage?

   What is God saying or revealing to you through this passage? In prayer, ask God what you can learn from this passage.

5. Write your own prayer letter to God, describing how you feel about the passage. Write about insights or inspirations you have gained. Include doubts, fears, or questions that this passage has inspired.

Retreats for Teens

The FRIEND

You have fifty cents to spend. Mark on the lines how much you are willing to spend for the qualities you would like to see in a friend.

My ideal friend...

_____ wears the right clothes

_____ has a nice smile

_____ is affectionate

_____ is good looking

_____ has plenty of money

_____ is intelligent

_____ has a good personality

_____ is compassionate

_____ is generous

_____ has artistic ability

_____ is open and honest

_____ has spiritual depth

_____ shares common interests with me

_____ has good connections

_____ is trustworthy

_____ has a great body

_____ is patient

_____ lives in a big house

_____ is popular

_____ has musical ability

_____ is loyal

_____ is gentle

_____ lives according to moral convictions

_____ is kind

_____ is a good listener

_____ likes to party

_____ is humble

_____ is honest

_____ has a good sense of humor

_____ is forgiving

_____ has lots of time

_____ is dependable

_____ has athletic ability

_____ lives close to me

_____ is very talented

_____ is my age

_____ has a nice family

_____ is faithful

Line-ups

Where do you stand? Left, right, or somewhere in the middle? Listen to these descriptions and when you hear the word "Go," line up at the place that best describes you.

Morning person _____ Night person

- jumps out of bed, ready to go
- likes to tackle important projects early in the day
- enjoys having breakfast with friends

- needs caffeine for a jump-start
- likes to sleep in
- works best after 9:00 pm
- can't face food or friends until noon

Picky Eater _____ Eats anything

- is suspicious of any new food
- can't stand one food touching another on his or her plate
- packs peanut butter for emergencies

- will try anything, at least once
- thinks potlucks are great fun

People Person _____ Private Person

- is almost never alone
- feels energized by being in large groups of people
- likes activities that involve lots of noise and people

- is comfortable being alone
- feels tense and uncertain in big gatherings
- likes quiet activities that involve being alone—writing, reading, walking

Leader _____ Follower

- likes to be in charge
- is able to motivate others
- has strong preferences

- likes to be part of a team or group
- is comfortable going with the flow
- can be flexible about preferences

Listener _____ Talker

- is genuinely interested in what others have to say
- pays attention to other people's stories
- asks questions and waits to hear the answers

- finds it difficult to be quiet and listen
- is eager to add his or her own comments to others' stories
- plans what he or she will say next while others are talking

Line-ups

Walking in the school hallway I usually...

▲   ▲   ▲

say "Hi" to everyone I meet   say "Hi" only   try not to make eye
                            to people I know   contact with anyone

At a party I usually...

▲   ▲   ▲

stick with my friends   reach out to at least   try to talk to everyone
                            one new person

In playing a game, I usually...

▲   ▲   ▲

play by the rules   take some calculated risks   pull out all the stops

When I meet someone new, I usually...

▲   ▲   ▲

take the initiative   respond to the other   feel disappointed when the
                        person's initiative   other person makes no
                                                effort to get acquainted

How Do I Build My Friendships?

RISKING

CARING

LISTENING

TRUSTING

SHARING

➤ Number the five building blocks of friendship in order of their importance to you.

➤ In each box write the name or initial of someone who exemplifies the quality.

➤ Which quality is the weakest or is lacking in your friends right now? Put an "✘" through that building block.

➤ Which quality is the strongest or is demonstrated most clearly by your friends right now? Put a "★" in that building block.

➤ Write brief answers to the following questions: Thinking of my present friendships, the most important thing that my friends and I did to build our friendships was to….

In times of trouble I turn to….

The person who has influenced me most is….

The person who has influenced me most in positive ways is….

The person who builds me up is….

The person who accepts me for who I am is….

Pray.com

How to Spend Fifteen Minutes in Prayer

• That's half the length of a TV show! • How can anyone pray for fifteen minutes?
• What will I say? • What if I fall asleep? • Won't God get tired of me?

Prayer is a communicating with God. As friends grow closer through their sharing, so we grow closer to God through the time we spend in prayer. Making prayer a part of your life can change your life.

Of course, you can talk to God any way you like, but here's a suggestion for a fifteen-minute conversation with God.

> **P**raise God (two minutes)
> **R**epent (two minutes)
> **A**sk God about your needs (two minutes)
> **Y**ours: talk about family, friends, others, the world (four minutes)
> **.** (dot) listen (five minutes)
> **com**munication continues

Praise God—Begin your prayer with a recognition of God's greatness. Jesus gave us a model for this recognition when he began, "Our Father in heaven, hallowed be your name" (Matthew 6:9). This is your time to praise God for who he is (Psalm 63:3-4). After a minute of praise, take another minute to thank God for what he has done in your life and in the world. Be specific about what you are thankful for—you shouldn't run out of things to list (Philippians 4:6, Psalm 100:4).

Repent (confess)—Tell God about your unconfessed sins. God won't be surprised, so don't hold back. A forgiven heart is a pure heart and prepares you for intimacy with God (Psalm 139:23-24, Psalm 51:10, 2 Corinthians 5:17-21, 1 John 1:9).

Ask God—This part of prayer is usually easy for us. We're pretty good at letting God know what we think we want or need. Let God know the desires of your heart and the areas of your life that concern you (Matthew 7:7, Matthew 6:11).

Yours—Think about all the "yours" in your life: your family, friends, neighbors, community, world. Take time to pray (intercede) for them and for your world. Remember the prayer requests of your friends and family and make them known to God. Ask God to give you the name of someone who you can encourage today (1 Timothy 2:1-2, Psalm 2:8, Matthew 9:37-38, James 5:13-16).

. (dot) Listen—Take time to be quiet in God's presence. Use this time to listen for God's voice (Psalm 37:7, Isaiah 40:31). Also spend time reading Scripture and meditating on God's word.

Communication —Remember to pray always, to make conversation with God part of your daily life, and not something you do only in times of need (Luke 18:1-8, 1 Timothy 6:11-12). Strengthen your connection with a community of believers who will support you and hold you accountable to live as a Christian (Acts 2:42-44, 2 Corinthians 6:14-16).

Reconciliation Service

Forgiven

Materials: A block of wood that has sturdy three-dimensional letters glued on it to spell "forgiven" • a pan large enough to hold enough sand to cover the block of wood with about an inch of sand and leave two or three inches of empty space at the top • sand

Preparation: Secure the block of wood to the bottom of the pan and cover the sign with about an inch of sand.

If teens will have the opportunity to celebrate the sacrament of Penance with individual confessions, take time before the service to go over the logistics—where the priest(s) will be, how participants should line up and wait, what they should do when it is their turn, what they should do after their confession. Allow as much time as necessary to answer all questions. If possible, provide copies of *A Time and Place for Healing: The Sacrament of Penance for Teens* for teens to read ahead of time. See Appendix page 96.

INTRODUCTORY RITES

Song

Choose an appropriate song, one that your group knows and that fits with the service.

Suggestions: "Change My Heart, O God" from the CD *WOW Worship: Today's 30 Most Powerful Worship Songs*, Integrity • "Create New Hearts" from the CD *Find Us Ready*, Oregon Catholic Press, 800-548-8749 • "Gather Your People" from the CD *Alleluia, Give the Glory*, Oregon Catholic Press • "You Are Near" from the CD *Always and Everywhere*, Oregon Catholic Press

Note: If this service will include the celebration of the sacrament of Penance, it would be appropriate for the retreat team to meet with the priest who will celebrate to decide who will do the various parts of the service. If the service will not include the sacrament, the retreat director and other retreat team members can take the various parts.

Greeting

Opening Prayer

CELEBRATION OF THE WORD OF GOD

First Reading: Deuteronomy 30:11-20

Psalm Response: Psalm 51

Response: Lord, cleanse me from my sin.

Gospel Acclamation: John 8:12

Gospel: John 8:1-11

Homily (Based on thoughts from the readings)

Note: Following are suggestions that the priest or retreat team members can use or adapt.

EXAMINATION OF CONSCIENCE

Let us reflect on the times when we turned away from God's commands. When have we allowed our hearts to be led astray? When have we sought our own selfish pleasures in thoughts and actions? What choices and decisions have we made that did not bring life? When have we cast stones at others? Have we taken the time to see the sin in our own lives? What do we need to bring before the Lord today for his forgiveness?

RITE OF RECONCILIATION

General Confession of Sins

All: My God, I am sorry for my sins with all my heart. In choosing to do wrong and in failing to do good, I have sinned against you and your church. I firmly intend, with your help, to do penance, to sin no more, and to avoid whatever leads me to sin. Our Savior Jesus Christ suffered and died for us. In his name, my God, have mercy. Amen

All: The Lord's Prayer

Individual Confession and Absolution

When you are ready, please move to the reconciliation room. After you have received the sacrament, write a symbol of your sin in the sand. Then wipe your sin away until you find the message that is there for you. When you have seen the message, cover it with sand again so that the next person can discover it as well.

Please use the quiet time after you have received the sacrament for prayer, journaling, or writing a letter to Jesus. Above all, respect everyone's need for quiet.

Note: Ask a member of the retreat team to stand near the sand to be sure that the process is working correctly.

If teens will not have the opportunity to celebrate the sacrament of Penance, participants can recite a prayer of contrition or sorrow after the homily. Then use one of the following options to have participants receive the message that they have been forgiven. At the end of this service, remind teens that this was a nonsacramental service and let them know when and where the sacrament is available to them.

Option 1

A retreat team member is seated on a low stool or pillow at a low table with the pan of sand on it. Person A comes forward and sits across from the team member. Person A draws a symbol for his or her sin in the sand, and the retreat team member wipes it away to reveal the message from the Lord, covers the message with sand, and gets up.

Person A takes the place of the team member and waits for the next person (B) to come forward and draw a symbol for his or her sin in the sand. Person A wipes it away, covers the message with sand, and gets up. Person B waits for the next person (C). The process continues until everyone has had chance to read the message.

Option 2

Set the sand on a low table. As they are ready, participants take turns drawing symbols of their sins in the sand and then wiping the symbols away until they uncover the message. After reading the message, each is to cover the message with sand again, and return to his or her place.

Note: If you feel the group is mature enough, add this step. After each has drawn a symbol in the sand, ask that person to explain the symbol. Someone might say, for example, "I drew a mouth with a line through it because I need to be forgiven for gossiping." Or, "I drew a cloud with rain and a bolt of lightning because I need forgiveness for venting my anger at others."

CONCLUDING RITES

Sign of Peace

Final Blessing and Prayer

Closing Song

Choose an appropriate song, one that your group knows and that fits with the service.

Suggestions: "Hope to Carry On" and "Step by Step" from the CD *Songs 2: Rich Mullins*, Reunion • "In the Light" from the CD *In the Light: The Very Best of Charlie Peacock*, Re-Think • "Did You Feel the Mountains Tremble?" from the CD *Passion: The Road to One Day*, Sparrow Records

Retreat Evaluation

Please use the following numbers to rate your retreat experience. Thank you!

1 = Awesome!   **2 = Okay**   **3 = So-So**   **4 = Bad news!**

1. I rate the overall retreat experience as a _____ because _____
_____ .

2. I rate the Reconciliation Service as a _____ because _____
_____ .

3. I rate my attitude and my contribution to the experience as a _____ because _____
_____ .

4. I benefited from this retreat experience by being able to _____
_____
_____ .

5. For me, the highlight(s) of this retreat were _____
_____ .

That's because _____
_____ .

6. I'd like to suggest these themes and topics for future retreats. _____
_____

I have these suggestions to improve future retreats. _____
_____

7. I'd like to share these comments with the retreat team. _____

_____

8. I'd like to come to another retreat as a team member because _____

_____ .

9. I would not like to be a retreat team member. That's because _____

_____ .

Name (optional) _____

(Please be sure to include your name if you'd like to become a retreat team member. Feel free to continue your comments in the space below.)

Weekend Retreat

Sample Letter to Parents

(parish letterhead)

_____ *date*

Dear _____ *parent's or parents' name* _____,

We welcome you and your teen to the _____ *parish name and title of retreat* _____,
which will take place at _____ *time* _____ on _____ *date* _____, at
_____ *name and location of retreat center* _____.

We hope that the retreat weekend will be spiritually rewarding for all involved. We need your assistance and support to help insure that your teen will have a successful retreat experience.

There will be a special forty-five-minute meeting for parents at _____ *time* _____
on _____ *date* _____. The meeting will be held in the _____ *location of meeting* _____.
At this meeting, you will learn what is planned for the weekend, and you will have a chance to ask any questions you may have. If you will be attending the meeting, please call the office at
_____ *phone number* _____ to let me know that I can expect you.

At a very special time during the retreat, we will present your teen with a letter from a very important person—YOU! This is an excellent and unique opportunity for you to express your love for your teen and your feelings about your faith. The opportunity to convey a positive, loving message to your teen doesn't come along often enough, yet everyone needs to be told how much he or she is loved and appreciated! These letters of affirmation, support, and encouragement are literally love letters from home, and it is important that each retreat participant receive at least one letter.

The love letters are meant to be a surprise for the teens, so please keep your letter a secret. Seal your letter in an envelope addressed to your son or daughter and marked with a "P" in the upper-right-hand corner to identify it as a letter from a parent. Please deliver your letter to the parish office no later than _____ *date* _____. If you want to mail the letter, put it into another envelope and send it to me at the parish address.

Please encourage other family members and friends to write letters, also to be given to your teen during the weekend. We would like each participant to have at least two extra letters, again sealed in envelopes addressed to your son or daughter. These letters do not need a special marking, but they also will be a surprise.

The cost for the weekend is $____.__ for each teen. We ask that fees be paid by _____*date*_____.

Transportation to and/or from the retreat center weekend is also needed. Please consider volunteering to drive on Friday night, Sunday afternoon, or both. It is only a ___-minute drive. Teens will not be allowed to drive their own vehicles. If you can help, please return the transportation form along with the permission and health forms.

All participants will leave the church parking lot as a group on Friday night and return as a group on Sunday. We ask that your teen arrive at the parking lot on Friday night, _____*date*_____, no later than _____ pm. On Sunday, _____*date*_____, we will leave the retreat center around _____ pm, arriving at the parking lot by _____ pm.

Dinner will not be served on Friday evening so please make sure your teen has had something to eat. Please notify us if your teen has any special medical needs, medication that he or she needs to take, or dietary requirements. It is important that the retreat team be made aware of any out-of-the-ordinary situations. The permission and health forms included in this letter are to be returned by _____*date*_____. You may bring the forms to the parent meeting, drop them off at the parish office, or mail them to my attention at the parish.

With this letter is an informational letter for your teen. Please pass this on to your son or daughter so that he or she will know what to expect and what to bring. Also included is a copy of the Retreat Guidelines that will be given to your teen at the retreat center on Friday evening. Please take the time to review these with your teen.

Participants will not be allowed to leave at any time during the weekend. Late arrivals on Friday may be allowed on an individual basis. Call me at least two weeks before the retreat for approval.

Finally, and most importantly, we ask you to pray for the success of this retreat. God's work depends upon the prayers and support of his people. We are hoping that God will touch your teen's life in a special and unique way during this retreat.

Thank you for supporting us in the youth ministry programs! If you have questions, please call.

In Peace,

_____

Signature

Title

Enclosures:
Permission and health forms, to be returned by _____*date*_____.
Letter for Teens
Retreat Guidelines
Transportation form, to be returned by _____*date*_____.

Weekend Retreat

Permission Form
Parent/Legal Guardian Permission and Indemnity Agreement

For a retreat at _____
name of retreat center

_____
complete address and phone number, including phone number for emergencies

Child/Ward _____

Parish/School _____

Designated supervisor of activity _____

Description of activity _____

Dates and time of activity _____

Method of transportation _____

Cost (if applicable) _____

I consent to the participation of my child/ward in the above-named activity. In consideration for my child/ward's participation, I agree to reimburse and indemnify the parish/school (understood to include the diocese of _____) for all reasonable legal and court fees incurred by parish/school in defending a lawsuit that I or my child/ward may bring against parish/school, which relates to the above named activity if the parish/school is found not legally liable by the courts and prevails in the lawsuit. If the parish/school is found legally liable for injuries sustained by child/ward, this paragraph will not apply.

I certify that I have an understanding of this agreement and any risks and hazards associated with the activity described above that my child/ward will be participating in. I further understand that I had the opportunity to fully discuss this agreement with a representative of the parish/school to clarify any concerns or questions about the activity or this agreement that I may have had.

_____   _____
signature of parent/legal guardian   *date*

_____   _____
home phone   *work phone*

_____
address, including city, state, and zip code

EMERGENCY MEDICAL TREATMENT

In the event of an emergency, I give permission to transport my child to a hospital for emergency medical treatment. I wish to be advised prior to any further treatment by the hospital or doctor. In the event of an emergency, if you are unable to reach me at the above numbers, contact:

Name _____

Phone Number _____

Please furnish medical information about your child/ward, which may be pertinent to his or her participation in the above-identified activity: _____

_____

. . . .

FOR RETREAT PARTICIPANT*

I have read the Retreat Guidelines and understand that if I violate the trust placed in me, my parents will be contacted immediately and will be asked to pick me up.

_____
signature of retreat participant

*Your signature here is required before you will be allowed to participate in the retreat.

PLEASE RETURN BY _____

Weekend Retreat

Health Form

NAME_____ SEX _____ BIRTHDATE _____

ADDRESS _____ PHONE _____

CITY _____ STATE _____ ZIP _____

PARISH/SCHOOL/GROUP _____

FAMILY PHYSICIAN OR CLINIC _____

PHONE _____

FAMILY HEALTH INSURANCE _____

POLICY NUMBER _____

Please list any health information that might be needed by the retreat team or emergency personnel: allergies or other chronic conditions, recent or current illness or injury, tetanus status, and so on. _____

_____

_____

_____

Please list any medications that your teen will be taking while on retreat.

_____

_____

_____

The following can be given to my teen if it is necessary (as prescribed on the product label):

❏ Tylenol   ❏ Ibuprofen   ❏ Aspirin

_____   _____
signature of parent(s)   *date*

Weekend Retreat

Sample Letter to Teens
(parish letterhead)

_____ *date* _____

Dear _____ ,

We are happy to welcome you to this retreat, _____ *title of retreat* _____ .

Whether this your first retreat or whether you have experienced other retreats, there are certain things you need to know in order to prepare for this very special weekend.

When is the retreat?

Friday, _____ *date* _____, at _____ *time* _____, through Sunday, _____ *date* _____, at _____ *time* _____ .

Where will the retreat be held?

_____ *name and location of retreat center* _____

What will you need to bring?*

Towels, soap, toothpaste, toothbrush, and other personal items
A sleeping bag or bedding. A bed and pillow are provided.
Comfortable clothes for indoors and out
Your Bible
Your own soda, juice or snacks. Please label them with your name.
An open heart and mind

What should you NOT bring?

Radios
TV
Tape or CD players
Head phones
Cell phones
Pagers
Laser pointers
School books

> You will not need any of these items. If you bring them, they will be collected and returned to you at the end of the weekend.
>
> In addition, the possession of DRUGS, TOBACCO PRODUCTS, ALCOHOL, and/or other INTOXICANTS are forbidden. Anyone who brings any of these items, or gives evidence of using any of these items, will be asked to leave immediately. Your parents will be contacted and will be asked to pick you up.

*This list may need to be modified to fit your situation.

Retreats for Teens

Where will we be meeting?

_____

At what time?

No later than _____ pm

> Please eat before you arrive. Dinner will not be provided on Friday night, although a light snack will be served later in the evening.

What time will we be returning?

_____

What if someone needs to come late or leave during some portion of the retreat?

No one will be allowed to miss any portion of the retreat. Conflicts that cause late arrival on Friday will be taken into consideration. To get approval for a late arrival, please call _____*name*_____, the retreat director, at _____*phone number*_____, at least two weeks before the retreat. Please don't hesitate to call with other questions you may have.

Retreats are unique and rewarding experiences. We can promise that this retreat will be well worth your time and effort. Remember, you'll get out of the retreat what you put into it. Retreats are not done to you or for you, they involve you! We look forward to seeing you on _____*date*_____.

Until then, please keep the retreat team and the other retreat participants in your prayers.

Peace,

signature of the retreat director or director of youth ministry
title

signatures of the retreat team, with their titles

Weekend Retreat

Sample Retreat Guidelines*

No running in the building.

Keep rooms neat.

Snacks and soda are not allowed in dormitories due to health laws (and to prevent the presence of little critters). You may bring your own soda and snacks, provided they are labeled with your name and stored in the area designated for snacks.

Keep noise down.

All furnishings must stay in the rooms in which they were found.

No guys in the girls' dorm. No girls in the guys' dorm. At any time!

No one will be allowed outdoors on Friday night. There will be time for outdoor activities on Saturday and Sunday.

If you need anything or if you feel sick, ask any retreat member for help.

There is a curfew each night because a good night's sleep will be essential for keeping up with the weekend's busy schedule. Please cooperate when you are asked to turn the lights out, and respect others' right to sleep. Those who abuse this guideline will be asked to leave. Their parents will be called and asked to pick them up.

NO DRUGS, TOBACCO PRODUCTS, ALCOHOL, or other INTOXICANTS! Anyone possessing or using any of these items will be sent home immediately—no matter what time of day or night!

Please do not bring radios, TVs, tape players, CD players, head phones, cell phones, pagers, laser pointers, or school books. The full schedule for this weekend will not allow time for school work. Activities scheduled for free time and breaks are intended to encourage interaction and community building among participants.

God has called you to this retreat. Allow God to work in you and through you. Be open and honest. Be yourself!

*Add items that are necessary for the site you are using and for your group.

Weekend Retreat

Transportation Form

_____ *retreat title*

_____ *date*

_____ *location of retreat*

_____ *complete address and phone number of retreat center*

Please check all that apply.

❏ I am able to drive teens to the retreat center at _____ on _____ .

❏ I am able to pick teens up at the retreat center at _____ on _____ .

❏ I am able to do both.

I am able to take a total of _____ passengers, not including myself. (Note: Number of passengers can equal the number of sets of seat belts available.)

Name _____ Phone _____

Please return on or before _____

Thank you!

Resources

For additional help in planning retreats for teens, see the following resources available from Pflaum Publishing Group, Dayton, OH 45439 (800-543-4383).

Ciernick, Bernard and Louise Santiago, *The All-Purpose, Hands-On Confirmation Director's Manual.* Offers three models for Confirmation retreats.

Dotterweich, Kass, *Making Connections: 25 Stories for Sharing Faith with Teens.* Includes reflection questions for each story.

Durback, Christina Bigatel, *FAQs About Confirmation: What You Want To Know.* Answers questions commonly asked by Confirmation candidates, their parents, and sponsors.

Forgiveness and Healing. (One of eight books in the youth ministry series, *Conversations with Teens: Catholic Perspectives.*) Offers models for reconciliation services.

Giombi, Gary, *Paths of Prayer: A Textbook of Prayer and Meditation.* Suggests a wide variety of prayer experiences for teens.

Givens, Steve, *A Time and Place for Healing: The Sacrament of Penance for Teens.* Provides a straightforward, concise explanation of the meaning and benefits of this sacrament.

Riedel, Patty Hupfer, *Getting Started: 100 Icebreakers for Youth Gatherings.*

Visit us at www.Pflaum.com